Jan Nowak
Editor

Marketing in Central and Eastern Europe

Pre-publication
REVIEWS,
COMMENTARIES,
EVALUATIONS . . .

Former communist countries have never been as homogenous as many Western analysts have maintained. With the collapse of communism and the emergence of different cultures, political-historical traditions, and transformation strategies, even more sophisticated analyses are called for. The book leads us into a more advanced stage of understanding the theoretical and practical marketing challenges facing Western academics and businessmen in postcommunist markets. It does so by presenting more rigorous analyses and hypotheses testing. The book deserves to be read by all the serious students of these emerging markets

Val Samonis, PhD, CPC
Professor of East-West Business and Transition Economics, University of Toronto; Member, Economic Transition Group, Stanford University

International Business Press
An Imprint of The Haworth Press, Inc.

Marketing in Central and Eastern Europe

The East-West Business series:

The Central and Eastern European Markets: Guideline for New Business Ventures, edited by Petr Chadraba

East-West Business Relationships: Establishment and Development, edited by Jarmo Nieminen

Marketing in Central and Eastern Europe, edited by Jan Nowak

These books were published simultaneously as special thematic issues of the *Journal of East-West Business* and are available bound separately. For further information, call 1-800-HAWORTH (outside US/Canada: 607-722-5857), Fax 1-800-895-0582 (outside US/Canada: 607-771-0012) or e-mail getinfo@haworth.com

Marketing in Central and Eastern Europe

Jan Nowak
Editor

International Business Press
An Imprint of
The Haworth Press, Inc.
New York • London

Published by

International Business Press, 10 Alice Street, Binghamton, NY 13904-1580 USA

International Business Press is an imprint of The Haworth Press, Inc., 10 Alice Street, Bing-hamton, NY 13904-1580 USA.

Marketing in Central and Eastern Europe has also been published as *Journal of East-West Business*, Volume 3, Number 1 1996.

The development, preparation, and publication of this work has been undertaken with great care. However, the publisher, employees, editors, and agents of The Haworth Press and all imprints of The Haworth Press, Inc., including The Haworth Medical Press and Pharmaceutical Products Press, are not responsible for any errors contained herein or for consequences that may ensue from use of materials or information contained in this work. Opinions expressed by the author(s) are not neces-sarily those of The Haworth Press, Inc.

Cover design by Donna Brooks

Library of Congress Cataloging-in-Publication Data

Marketing in Central and Eastern Europe / Jan Nowak, editor.
      p. cm.
      "Has also been published as Journal of East-West Business, volume 3, number 1, 1996"–T.p. verso.
      Includes bibliographical references and index.
      ISBN 0-7890-0039-3 (alk. paper)
      1. Marketing–Europe, Eastern. 2. Marketing–Europe, Central. I. Nowak, Jan.
HF5415.12.E815M37 1997
658.8′00947–dc21
                                          97-762
                                          CIP

INDEXING & ABSTRACTING

Contributions to this publication are selectively indexed or abstracted in print, electronic, online, or CD-ROM version(s) of the reference tools and information services listed below. This list is current as of the copyright date of this publication. See the end of this section for additional notes.

- *CNPIEC Reference Guide: Chinese National Directory of Foreign Periodicals,* P.O. Box 88, Beijing, People's Republic of China

- *Contents Pages in Management,* University of Manchester Business School, Booth Street West, Manchester M15 6PB, England

- *GEO Abstracts (GEO Abstracts/GEOBASE),* Elsevier/ GEO Abstracts, Regency House, 34 Duke Street, Norwich NR3 3AP, England

- *Guide to Social Science & Religion in Periodical Literature,* National Periodical Library, P.O. Box 3278, Clearwater, FL 34630

- *Human Resources Abstracts (HRA),* Sage Publications, Inc., 2455 Teller Road, Newbury Park, CA 91320

- *Index to Periodical Articles Related to Law,* University of Texas, 727 East 26th Street, Austin, TX 78705

- *INTERNET ACCESS (& additional networks) Bulletin Board for Libraries ("BUBL"), coverage of information resources on INTERNET, JANET, and other networks.*
  - JANET X.29: UK.AC.BATH.BUBL or 00006012101300
  - TELNET: BUBL.BATH.AC.UK or 138.38.32.45 login 'bubl'
  - Gopher: BUBL.BATH.AC.UK (138.32.32.45). Port 7070
  - World Wide Web: http: / / www.bubl.bath.ac.uk./BUBL/ home.html
  - NISSWAIS: telnetniss.ac.uk (for the NISS gateway)
  The Andersonian Library, Curran Building, 101 St. James Road, Glasgow G4 ONS, Scotland

(continued)

- *Management & Marketing Abstracts,* Pira International, Randalls Road, Leatherhead, Surrey KT22 7RU, England

- *Operations Research/Management Science,* Executive Sciences Institute, 1005 Mississippi Avenue, Davenport, IA 52803

- *Political Science Abstracts,* IFI/Plenum Data Company, 3202 Kirkwood Highway, Wilmington, DE 19808

- *Referativnyi Zhurnal (Abstracts Journal of the Institute of Scientific Information of the Republic of Russia),* The Institute of Scientific Information, Baltijskaja ul., 14, Moscow A-219, Republic of Russia

- *Sociological Abstracts (SA),* Sociological Absracts, Inc., P.O. Box 22206, San Diego, CA 92192-0206

SPECIAL BIBLIOGRAPHIC NOTES

*related to special journal issues (separates)
and indexing/abstracting*

❑ indexing/abstracting services in this list will also cover material in any "separate" that is co-published simultaneously with Haworth's special thematic journal issue or DocuSerial. Indexing/abstracting usually covers material at the article/chapter level.

❑ monographic co-editions are intended for either non-subscribers or libraries which intend to purchase a second copy for their circulating collections.

❑ monographic co-editions are reported to all jobbers/wholesalers/approval plans. The source journal is listed as the "series" to assist the prevention of duplicate purchasing in the same manner utilized for books-in-series.

❑ to facilitate user/access services all indexing/abstracting services are encouraged to utilize the co-indexing entry note indicated at the bottom of the first page of each article/chapter/contribution.

❑ this is intended to assist a library user of any reference tool (whether print, electronic, online, or CD-ROM) to locate the monographic version if the library has purchased this version but not a subscription to the source journal.

❑ individual articles/chapters in any Haworth publication are also available through the Haworth Document Delivery Services (HDDS).

ABOUT THE EDITOR

Jan Nowak, PhD, is Associate Professor of Business at the University of New Brunswick, Saint John, Canada, where he teaches marketing and international business. Dr. Nowak's research interest is international marketing, with a focus on marketing in Central and Eastern Europe. He has published two books and over a dozen articles in scholarly journals and has served as guest editor of the *Journal of East-West Business* and the *Journal of Euromarketing*.

Marketing in Central and Eastern Europe

CONTENTS

Preface

The demise of communism in the Post Command Economies (PCEs) has created considerable interest from both academics and practitioners. Many of those exploring the region, however, have failed to consider fundamental issues of cross-cultural inquiry. In particular those interested in the region should be considering issues related to commonality.

Prior to 1990 many businesses perceived the region as being relatively homogenous. However, emergent differences in national culture, coupled with fiscal and monetary autonomy of each nation, has resulted in a more complex market to evaluate and segment. One way researchers can determine commonality within the region is by utilizing multivariate interdependence analyses. Mueller and Mueller demonstrate how the employment of cluster and factor analyses can be used to identify more sub-groups of PCEs. Though the analyses used group countries together based on various economic and political variables, the emergent clusters largely reflect traditional geo-cultural sub-groupings: the Baltics, Central Europe, Eastern Europe, Russia and Peripheral, and Central Asia.

Though commonality among PCEs is important, commonality with non-PCEs is an equally important issue. Managerial and marketing research is in its infancy in most PCEs and there is little empirical evidence that suggests commonality in Western and PCE phenomena. Researchers and practitioners should be especially cautious, therefore, when using Western measures or assuming constructs (or strategies) developed in the West are applicable in PCEs. Those interested in researching PCE phenomena are encouraged to use the five step approach developed by Berry (1989).

[Haworth co-indexing entry note]: "Preface." Kaynak, Erdener. Co-published simultaneously in *Journal of East-West Business* (International Business Press, an imprint of The Haworth Press, Inc.) Vol. 3, No. 1, 1996, pp. xiii-xvii; and: *Marketing in Central and Eastern Europe* (ed: Jan Nowak) International Business Press, an imprint of The Haworth Press, Inc., 1996, pp. xi-xv. Single or multiple copies of this article are available for a fee from The Haworth Document Delivery Service [1-800-342-9678, 9:00 a.m. - 5:00 p.m. (EST). E-mail address: getinfo@haworth.com].

xi

Finally, much of the research carried out so far has been exploratory in nature. In particular, the ethnographic approach has often been employed. Though ethnography is important for exploring phenomena and developing hypotheses, more effort needs to be directed at testing hypotheses. The use of multivariate dependence analyses, such as confirmatory factor analyses, offers businesses and academics a powerful tool to investigate and test constructs.

Marketization and Westernization are advanced as two dimensions for classifying the countries of Central and Eastern Europe. Marketization refers to countries' dramatic exposure to global communications, increased product availability, and an overall attempt to close the living standards gap with the more developed countries. Westernization refers to the respective countries' proximity to the West and the duration and extent of their openness to Western influence. According to Lascu, Manrai and Manrai, these dimensions jointly provide marketing practitioners with criteria for segmentation that are culturally relevant to the region, as well as relevant to the process of transition to a market economy.

In terms of categorization, the Czech and Slovak Republics, Hungary, Poland and Slovenia belong to the high-marketization, high-Westernization quadrant, the countries of the former Yugoslavia (with the exception of Slovenia) belong to the low-marketization, high-Westernization quadrant, Bulgaria and Romania belong to the high marketization, low-Westernization quadrant, and Albania and the Western countries of the former Soviet Union belong to the low-marketization, low-Westernization quadrant. The article offers suggestions to marketing practitioners with regard to appropriate use of this classification for segmentation purposes.

The countries of Eastern and Central Europe have been progressing on the road to a market economy for a number of years now. U.K. companies, like other Western firms, aware of the region's inhabitants' pent-up desire for numerous consumer and industrial products and services, have invested significantly, although cautiously. The paper by Ali and Mirza focuses on U.K. foreign direct investment in Poland. It presents a cross sectional profile of U.K. firms investing in Poland, their motives for entering the Polish market, and their entry strategies, and assesses their performance in terms of their entry strategies and experiences with regard to financial, technological, marketing and strategic aspects. It proceeds to present preliminary findings which suggest that motives for investing in Poland are largely country specific, and firms prefer equity control in the investments. The paper concludes by suggesting implications for international market entry-theory.

From management perspective, the findings suggest that British companies' cautious attitude has paid off. Over two thirds of companies said that their investment expectations had been met or exceeded. This is good news for both existing and new investors in Poland, especially now that the country's economy is on a growth path. However, the initial risks in Poland and nearby East European countries (for which Poland may be an entry route) should not be underestimated by managers, who should learn from the early entrants. In this context, a close relationship with local entrepreneurs, in the form of joint venture and other co-operative links, should be explored, especially by new entrants.

Foreign direct investment (FDI) is a critical component in the growth of developing economies. The restructuring of the former Soviet Bloc countries into market-based economies provides Western firms with significant expansion opportunities. Rahman and Carpano analyze investment opportunities in one of the most promising Eastern European countries, Hungary. Specifically, they consider firm strategies in terms of FDI vis-à-vis Hungary's economic environment and country-specific factor endowments.

Relative to other Eastern European countries, Hungary has the greatest chance for economic success with respect to: (1) economic development potential (i.e., industry structure, infrastructure, skills, foreign debt, and exports in convertible currency), and (2) readiness and ability to change (i.e., commitment by people and leadership, and scope of reforms, experience with reforms, national homogeneity, quality of leadership, traditions/emotions). Because it started upon a privatization program while still under communist rule, it has the largest private sector in the region. Notwithstanding some controversy related to its privatization policy within the current Socialist government in early 1955, the political environment in Hungary is stable. Its primary factor endowments are related to a relatively high-skilled labor force that is paid significantly less than in Western countries, a pro-business environment in terms of property rights, environmental standards, and finance, and its proximity and potential access to the lucrative European Union market. An indication of Hungary's attractiveness as an FDI site is given by the fact that over 50% of the FDI inflow into Central Europe has gone to Hungary.

As may be expected, the FDI inflow to date has been mainly into manufacturing industries by firms interested in using Hungary as an export platform for the larger European market. These efficiency-seeking firms are attracted by Hungary's proximity to the European Union and its labor costs. However, since export-oriented FDI needs adequate infrastructure and service industries, it has stimulated FDI in those sectors from market-seeking firms. While we expect Hungary's labor cost advantage to deteriorate over time, efficiency-seeking firms will continue to benefit from using Hungary as an export platform in the high-end manufacturing industries.

The transitional economies of Central and Eastern European (CEE) countries can offer unique and diverse challenges to theorists and practitioners attempting to apply Western business theory and experience to market situations that have not reached the West's state of maturity and experience. The direct transplantation of Western ideas does not always work in practice.

The purpose of the paper by Hill and Kennington is to assess whether marketing theory and practice developed in Western free-market economies, specifically the process and tools of strategic marketing, can be used to help guide the strategies of firms in such transitional economies. It reports on research conducted in Poland in 1994 on the marketing of personal banking products by Polish banks.

The study comprised three parts: interviews with senior Polish bankers to identity strategies, a survey of front-line staff to determine whether strategies had been communicated and reinforced in the reward system, and a consumer survey to determine whether the strategies had had successful outcomes. The results demonstrate that Polish bankers are using strategic marketing inconsistently and incompletely, and have failed to provide the staff training and changes to reward systems that might instill and reinforce a more customer-focused marketing orientation.

Particularly lacking are the key strategic concepts of marketing:

segmentation, targeting, positioning and marketing orientation. Consumers are picking up on the banks' efforts at marketing but it appears that the key criteria on which customers choose banks and the "wish list" they have for bank service are being virtually ignored by the banks when setting strategies. The consumer study did, however, identity some differentiable market segments with specific needs and potential positioning platforms.

Overall, the research finds that the concepts and tools of Western-style marketing can provide direction to bankers for strategy setting, but that successful implementation will depend on the adaptation of these concepts to the specific context.

Erdener Kaynak
Editor
Journal of East-West Business

REFERENCE

Berry, J.W. (1989). "Imposed Etics-Emic-Derived Etics: The Operationalization of a Compelling Idea," *International Journal of Psychology*, Vol. 24, pp. 721-735.

Introduction

Since the sudden opening up of the markets in Central and Eastern Europe (CEE) in 1989, there has been a growing need to investigate the fundamental changes occurring in the countries' marketing environment, the lucrative market opportunities created by the changes, and the inscrutable marketing practice followed by local and international companies. The need has been especially acute for scholarly research aimed at gaining an understanding of the specificity of the CEE marketing phenomena and the necessity to deal with these phenomena in a region-specific and transformation-specific manner. Although a myriad of studies may seem to have been undertaken by Western scholars and their Eastern counterparts, the issues are far from being overstudied. In fact, there are still significant gaps in our knowledge and understanding of how marketing processes shape up in Central and Eastern Europe. These gaps are not easily fillable due to the ongoing economic, social, technological and political transformation which is underway in the region and which constantly produces new challenges and opportunities. The purpose of this volume is to provide a forum for discussion of the changes in the marketing environment and marketing practice in the CEE countries, and of the methodological requirements for effective and unbiased research into these changes. In its practical dimension, the volume is intended to provide Western companies with a better understanding of the emerging opportunities and effective marketing strategies to be employed in the region. The following five papers have been selected to contribute to the pursuance of this purpose.

In the first paper, which provides a context and guidelines for conducting research into marketing phenomena of the region under consideration, Drs. R. D. Mueller and J. D. Mueller address two fundamental and related issues of commonality among post-command economies (PCEs)

[Haworth co-indexing entry note]: "Introduction." Nowak, Jan. Co-published simultaneously in *Journal of East-West Business* (International Business Press, an imprint of The Haworth Press, Inc.) Vol. 3, No. 1, 1996, pp. 1-6; and: *Marketing in Central and Eastern Europe* (ed: Jan Nowak) International Business Press, an imprint of The Haworth Press, Inc., 1996, pp. 1-6. Single or multiple copies of this article are available for a fee from The Haworth Document Delivery Service [1-800-342-9678, 9:00 a.m. - 5:00 p.m. (EST). E-mail address: getinfo@haworth.com].

1

and commonality between these economies and the Western world. When addressing the first issue, the authors challenge the validity of the East European construct, arguing that the region is no longer homogeneous and requires segmentation into sub-regions exhibiting important geo-cultural similarities. Based on multivariate interdependence analyses, the authors distinguish five emergent clusters–the Baltics, Central Europe, Eastern Europe, Russia and Peripheral, and Central Asia. When addressing the second issue, the authors caution researchers and practitioners, who derive their expertise from Western theory and practice, that what may hold true in Western cultures may not hold true in the post-communist countries. Then they offer suggestions for testing equivalence of marketing constructs across cultures in order to increase the validity of research results and effectiveness of marketing programs in the PCEs. In conclusion, they make an insightful statement arguing that immediately after the collapse of the command system, exploratory research was necessary to aid our understanding of business phenomena in the PCEs. Now, they suggest, it is time to move to more rigorous analyses and hypotheses testing.

The issue of clustering or segmenting Central and East European countries is also addressed, although from a different angle, by the second paper. Drs. D. Lascu, L. Manrai and A. Manrai use marketization and Westernization as the two dimensions for clustering the CEE countries. They argue that these dimensions are more relevant and hence more useful for marketing practitioners than economic development and culture. In that sense, this is an alternative approach to clustering the region's countries to that demonstrated in the first paper. By marketization the authors mean the countries' dramatic exposure to global communications, increased product availability and variety, and overall attempt to close the living standards gap with developed countries. Westernization, on the other hand, refers to the respective countries' proximity to the West and the duration and extent of their openness to Western influence. When using these two dimensions, the authors arrive at the following four clusters: the Czech and Slovak Republics, Hungary, Poland and Slovenia belong to the high-marketization, high-Westernization cluster; the countries of the former Yugoslavia (with the exception of Slovenia) belong to the low-marketization, high-Westernization cluster; Bulgaria and Romania make up the high-marketization and low-Westernization cluster; and Albania and the Western countries of the former Soviet Union form the low-marketization, low-Westernization cluster. The clusters are likely to have certain common characteristics and share similar consumer needs and purchasing behaviour. They capture simultaneously the dimensions of economic development, culture, history, and the degree of market reform. Therefore, the clusters can be used by marketing practitioners to differentiate between the countries in the region and can aid in making entry and marketing-mix decisions. For example, the first cluster would appear to be most attractive to international marketers; it has few impediments to foreign investment and ownership, comparatively high consumer purchasing power, and more urbanized areas. Also, because of the religious and ethnic consistency, cluster one is more susceptible to regiocentric strategies, permitting more standardized products and uniform promotion messages.

It is generally believed that a smooth transition to a market economy and sound economic growth of CEE nations would be difficult to achieve without external investment, which brings with it much-needed management skills, technical know-how and access to distribution channels of the West. The next two papers analyse the foreign investment environment, opportunities and strategies of investors in two countries of the region: Poland and Hungary. Both countries belong to the cluster characterized by the most advanced reforms towards a market economy and comparatively high levels of foreign investment or, to use the previous paper's terminology–by high marketization and high Westernization. Therefore, the two cases may be of particular interest to potential entrants into this cluster.

Professors S. Ali and H. Mirza examine entry strategies into the Polish market by U.K. firms, which have made significant investments in Central and Eastern Europe, although they have penetrated the region's markets more cautiously than their German counterparts. The article presents the results from a survey of a cross-section of British firms which have entered the Polish market. In particular, it focuses on their motives for entering this market, the nature of entry strategies chosen, and the companies' performance with regard to financial and marketing aspects. It is interesting to observe that the most common reason for investing in Poland chosen by respondents was Poland being "a strategic location." Indeed, Western firms seem to choose Poland not only because of its comparatively large market but perhaps more so due to its favourable geographic location vis-à-vis both powerful Western economies (Germany), and largely untapped and still highly risky Eastern markets (former Soviet Republics). Another interesting finding is that more than 60% of the firms have eventually established wholly owned subsidiaries, and that licensing was not used at all. The latter finding is in sharp contrast with the popularity of licensing in the pre-1990 period, when, on the one hand, it was very difficult if not impossible to make a direct investment and, on the other hand, strict import regulations as well as the chronic lack of hard currency made exporting fickle. The paper concludes by suggesting implications for international market-entry theory. It challenges the accepted model of internationalization process (the so-called Uppsala Model) according to which firms gradually proceed from low involvement to higher involvement modes of entry, pointing out that 40% of firms studied used majority equity modes as an initial entry method.

In the paper on investment conditions and opportunities in Hungary, Drs. M. Rahman and C. Carpano analyse firm foreign direct investment (FDI) strategies vis-à-vis Hungary's economic environment and country-specific factor endowments. The authors argue that Hungary is the preferred location for FDI among Eastern European countries, especially as an excellent export platform. This argument can be substantiated by the fact that between 1989 and 1995, over 50% of the FDI inflow into Central and Eastern Europe went to Hungary. It is predicted that Hungary will continue to be the favoured recipient of FDI in the region. Due to few resource endowments, Hungary is not attractive to resource-seeking firms. Due to its small market size, not very many market-seeking firms invest in this country either. However, Hungary's attractiveness to market-seeking firms is likely to increase in light of its expected membership in the EU. The strongest advantage of Hungary is its investment conditions–skilled yet inexpensive labour force, strong industrial tradition, good quality infrastructure, government incentives, political stability–which attract efficiency-seeking investors who tend to locate export-oriented operations in Hungary to capitalize on the country's proximity to other CEE markets and the EU.

The paper by J. Hill and C. Kennington is an example of sectorial analysis of marketing environments and strategies in the region under consideration. It addresses the issue of whether marketing theory and practice developed in Western market economies, specifically the process and tools of strategic marketing, can be also used in transitional economies. It reports results of a survey conducted in Poland in 1994 on the marketing of personal banking products by Polish banks. A series of interviews focused on overall marketing strategy, competitive advantage, segmentation, targeting and positioning, and the marketing orientation–the very pillars of Western-style marketing theory. Interestingly, the authors surveyed three groups of respondents–senior bank managers, front-line staff, and customers. The approach provided them with an opportunity to distinguish between strategy formulation and implementation and to confront the understanding and perception of the same

marketing phenomena as articulated by each of the three groups inter-
viewed. Another interesting aspect of the survey methodology is that the
researchers used mostly open-ended questions in order to avoid biasing
findings with Western preconceptions. The results indicate that the use of
strategic marketing is limited and generally non-differentiating (no segmentation, no positioning). There seems to be a lack of coherence in
strategic direction as communicated to staff. There is little evidence of
marketing orientation and a rather clear focus on "supply side." Banks'
utilization of the marketing-mix elements is patchy, with price and
promotion being the most conspicuous marketing variables used. The
consumer survey, however, provided insights that can be easily used in
an effective segmentation of the Polish personal banking market and in
clear positioning of banks' services therein. In fact, the research has
shown that the purchase behaviour of banking services in Poland does
not, in principle, differ from that in the West. Therefore, one is tempted to
conclude that what prevents Polish banks from researching their markets,
segmenting them appropriately, and positioning themselves according to
their competitive advantage, is mostly their inability to fully and consistently apply concepts and tools of modern strategic marketing.

Although each of the five papers addresses a specific topic and uses
different research approaches and methodologies, they seem to have
something in common: they do demonstrate that there is a great interest
in and an equally great need to scientifically investigate rapidly emerging
market opportunities, marketing-environment issues and marketing-strate-
gy problems with respect to transitional economies of Central and Eastern Europe. They also demonstrate that, when approached with caution,
methodological creativity, cross-cultural sensitivity, and deep understanding of the peculiarities and unique transitional situation of the region, Western-style research into marketing-related issues of CEE can
produce meaningful results, both from academic and managerial point of
view.

This volume would not have been possible without the initiative,
encouragement and guidance provided by Dr. Erdener Kaynak, the Editor of the *Journal of East-West Business*. I would also like to express my
appreciation to all the reviewers, who provided the authors with insightful comments and suggestions for improvement and, at the same time,
helped me with the difficult task of selecting only 5 papers from among
15 submitted. Professors Jerzy Dietl (University of Łódź, Poland),
Deirdre Grondin (University of New Brunswick, Canada), Larry Franko
(University of Massachusetts), Carolyn Kennington (University of Surrey, U.K.), Dana Lascu (University of Richmond), Wojciech Nasierow-

ski (University of New Brunswick), Jarmo Nieminen (Turku School of Economics and Business Administration, Finland), Stan Paliwoda (University of Calgary), Josef Poeschl (WIIW, Austria), Shelly Rhinehart (University of New Brunswick), Jan N. Saykiewicz (Duquesne University), Val Simonis (University of Toronto), Henryk Sterniczuk (University of New Brunswick), and Leon Zurawicki (University of Massachusetts) kindly agreed to review the manuscripts. Last but not least, I would like to thank all the authors who gave us the opportunity to consider their manuscripts, and to congratulate the authors whose papers are included in this collection.

Jan Nowak

Increasing the Validity
of Post Command Economy Research
and Application

Rene Dentiste Mueller
James D. Mueller

SUMMARY. The demise of communism in the post command economies (PCEs) has created considerable interest from both academics and practitioners. As a result, a myriad of Western marketing academics and practitioners have been exploring the region. Despite the abundance of literature on cross-cultural research and practice, many PCE researchers have failed to consider fundamental issues related to cross-cultural/cross-national research design. This paper highlights a number of problems researchers face when investigating PCE regional phenomena. In particular, the authors discuss the issue of commonality and demonstrate how the use of multivariate analy-

Rene Dentiste Mueller is Assistant Professor of Marketing at the College of Charleston. She served as a German linguist in the U.S. Military Intelligence Corps and has been involved in PCE studies since 1984. Since 1990, her academic focus has been on examining PCE marketing phenomena, in particular the changes in food distribution systems and, more recently, country of origin effects and consumer ethnocentricity.

James D. Mueller is Director of Student and Faculty Services and Assistant Professor at Thomas More College Crestview Hills, Kentucky. He served as a Russian linguist in the U.S. Military Intelligence Corps and has been researching various management phenomena in the PCE region. His most recent work has been identifying critical success factors within the process plant contracting industry.

[Haworth co-indexing entry note]: "Increasing the Validity of Post Command Economy Research and Application." Mueller, Rene Dentiste, and James D. Mueller. Co-published simultaneously in *Journal of East-West Business* (International Business Press, an imprint of The Haworth Press, Inc.) Vol. 3, No. 1, 1996, pp. 7-26; and: *Marketing in Central and Eastern Europe* (ed: Jan Nowak) International Business Press, an imprint of The Haworth Press, Inc., 1996, pp. 7-26. Single or multiple copies of this article are available for a fee from The Haworth Document Delivery Service [1-800-342-9678, 9:00 a.m. - 5:00 p.m. (EST). E-mail address: getinfo@haworth.com].

7

ses can be effectively used to: (1) identify more homogenous groupings of PCEs; and, (2) validate marketing constructs developed outside the PCEs. Though based on analyses of the interdependence of
political and economic variables, the authors identify sub-groupings
of countries that largely reflect traditional geo-cultural groupings:
the Baltics, Central Europe, Eastern Europe, Russia and Peripheral,
and Central Asia. The authors also discuss traditional cross-cultural
research approaches and demonstrate how the operationalisation of
appropriate approaches can improve the application of regional marketing strategy and validity of PCE findings. *[Article copies available
for a fee from The Haworth Document Delivery Service: 1-800-342-9678.
E-mail address: getinfo@haworth.com]*

INTRODUCTION

The demise of communism in the post command economies (PCEs) has
brought about many structural and organizational changes that have pro-
foundly affected the way and means of regional business practice. Some
have suggested that "the change in ordered dynamics" may have also
brought about a loss of conceptual clarity (Anon 1995). Indeed, that is one
reason that the region has become a major growth industry engaging both
the scholarly and policy communities (Terry 1993).

At a recent conference on the region,[1] European academics and practitioners reported on a variety of issues relating to the region. A recurring
theme throughout the conference proceedings and discussions related to
the applicability of Western theory and practice to the region. Many PCE
and non-PCE researchers were questioning the relevance of research and
practices based on measures and constructs developed in the West. Despite
the increased awareness of ethnocentric tendencies in business research
occurring across cultures and nations (e.g., Costa and Bamossy 1995,
Douglas et al. 1994; Berry et al. 1994), few researching the area seem to
fully consider methodological concerns related to cross-cultural or cross-
national research. As a result, findings are being challenged and academics
and practitioners alike are finding it difficult to defend positions, however
worthy.

A related methodological issue that receives much debate relates to
"commonality" and whether "universals" can be found in PCE regional
phenomena. The "unique" versus "universal" has been, and continues to
be, argued in almost all academic spheres–especially with regard to PCEs
(e.g., Savitt 1994; Pribova 1993; Kadar 1991). While both sides can be
argued convincingly, few have offered empirical evidence to support their
positions.

Both the "commonality" of phenomena and the "applicability" of Western research methods and practice throughout the region merit serious attention. It is not, however, evident that these issues receive the attention they deserve. The objective of this article is to examine the two issues by applying traditional cross-cultural methods and frameworks to PCE phenomena. By employing multivariate interdependence analyses, the authors demonstrate that the current "East European" construct is ill-defined; the region could be more effectively segmented into five sub-regions. The authors then review problems most marketers face when operating in the PCE region, recommend solutions to methodological problems, and suggest questions that readers might consider when reviewing PCE studies and findings.

THE EAST EUROPEAN CONSTRUCT

For the forty years following the end of the Second World War, the term "Eastern Europe" was used primarily to describe the various European countries which adhered to Marxist/Leninist principles: Albania, Bulgaria, Czechoslovakia, Eastern Germany, Hungary, Poland, Romania and Yugoslavia (Baeva 1991). This commonly held definition excluded Russia and the other European Soviet Republics. Apart from their military alliances, East European countries had several fundamental things in common which created a peculiar political economy: nationalization of the means of production and the imposition of rigid social and economic controls (Knox and Agnew 1989 p. 158). Nevertheless, the degree to which each country adhered to Soviet policy meant that there could be considerable differences between the countries.

The United Nations and other international organizations used a different name but categorized most of the East European nations similarly. The term Second World nations referred to the economic activity, technological know-how and role in the global economy shared by the East European members of COMECON,[2] except Yugoslavia (Staede 1978).

Others, however, define the East European construct based on cultural commonality. Since culture dictates much of an individual's, firm's and nation's behavior, discovering cultural commonality within the "East European" construct seems particularly worthwhile for marketers. Culturally, Eastern Europe might extend to Moscow as this is how far Napoleon's army and "European" influence traveled (Mellor 1975). One also might consider only the Eastern Orthodox Christian nations as being "Eastern Europe" with the Western Christian (Catholic and Protestant) being Central Europe. This would align Greece with Eastern Europe and the countries of the Baltics, Hungary and the Czech Republic, Poland and Slovakia with Central Europe. Regardless of whether the East European construct is of a political, economic, or cultural derivation, sub-constructs do appear to exist.

Poland, the Czech Republic, Slovakia, and Hungary have, since 1990, preferred to be called Central Europe–philosophically and psychologically distancing themselves from their socialist past. Since the break-away from the Soviet Union, the Baltic States have also been referring to themselves as Central Europe, citing similar geo-cultural arguments. In fact, many Central and East Europeans become offended when referred to as 'East European' because they feel the term has negative connotations and does not reflect their current Western-orientation.

As market researchers know, well-defined constructs are prerequisites for explaining and predicting phenomena (McDaniel and Gates 1993). However, the "East European" construct, as reviewed, is not well-defined; economists, historians, anthropologists and political scientists all use a diversity of groupings in describing the East European construct. As can be seen, each definition conveys a slightly different meaning (Table 1). Consequently, an early problem most researchers encounter relates to the definition of the region. How do we define a region where countries and their recent experiences are so intertwined and so similar yet at the same time so different? Are there any universal concepts of a regional or even sub-regional basis; is there, in fact, an East European construct?

Prior to 1990, there was much commonality in PCE marketing and business phenomena due to a similarly developed political economy. For example, the suppression of national culture, of political and economic autonomy, and competition, resulted in a system that allowed firms little control over their marketing mix (e.g., prices and production were set centrally, distribution channels controlled by the State and promotion used infrequently), which meant that PCE markets were perceived as being relatively homogenous by many non-PCE businesses. An abundance of literature, however, suggests that after years of forced assimilation, the former communist nations are actively re-establishing their identities (Applebaum 1994; Waltzer 1994; Marks 1994; and Burr 1993). Consequently, each nation might be considered an independent market.

Although collectively the PCE region represents one of the world's largest markets, Kadar (1991) correctly suggests that individually most PCEs are small countries with relatively small domestic markets and are insufficient for the effective development and operation of activities requiring extensive production, markets and resources. In circumstances like this, it is common for multi-national businesses to create larger sub-group-

TABLE 1. Some Common Terms Used to Define the East European Construct

Eastern Europe (excluding Soviet European republics)	Eastern Europe (including Soviet European republics)	Central and Eastern Europe (CEC)–often excludes Transcaucasian and Central Asian Republics
East and Central Europe (ECE) often excludes Transcaucasia and Central Asia Republics	Central Europe (Czech Republic, Hungary, Poland, Slovakia)	Central Europe (Czech Republic, Hungary, Poland, Slovakia and Baltic States)
Central Europe–(Czech Republic, Hungary, Poland, Slovakia, Baltic States, and former Yugoslavia)	Visegrad4 (Czech Republic, Hungary, Poland, Slovakia)	Former Centrally Planned Economies (FCPE) includes all countries leaving planned economic systems
Transitional Economies–includes all countries leaving planned economic systems	Former Soviet Bloc–all Central and East European and Soviet republics under the command economic system	Former Eastern Bloc–same as Former Soviet Bloc
Warsaw Pact–excludes Albania and former Yugoslavia	CMEA–Council for Mutual Economic Assistance. same as COMECON	COMECON–Bulgaria, Hungary, Poland, Romania, Czechoslovakia, USSR, Albania, East Germany, Mongolia, Cuba, Vietnam, and Yugoslavia (associate)
Former Soviet Union (FSU)	Commonwealth of Independent States (CIS)–all former Soviet countries except Georgia and the Baltics	Newly Independent States (NIS)–countries of the former Soviet Union

ings in order to achieve requisite critical mass and economies of scale for leverage with marketing programs and strategies (Jeannet and Hennessey 1992 p. 163). Better-defined regional sub-constructs could facilitate expansion of firms' product market, increase efficiency and help integrate operations into new and important markets. Though it might be more appropriate to rely on single country research, there is more demand for research findings that are applicable to a wider range of PCEs. Yet if we are to rely on wide market groupings, they must be viable.

The growth and popularity of regional economic groups such as GATT, EFTA, EU Visegrad, etc., provides some evidence of integrated transnational or supranational self-groupings which might aid businesses in devising marketing strategies. That many countries are actively seeking full membership status in these groups necessarily demands a certain amount of uniformity in business practices and outcomes due to such things as: quality control mandates and uniform product standards; packaging, branding and communications legislation impacting on communication programs and strategies; and competitive legislation dictating acceptable competitive behavior, store opening times, etc.

Figure 1 shows the most common pre-1990 groupings and the regrouping of countries based on a number of variables. For example, the IMF has grouped the nations into "clear and useful" groups based on economic reforms (Havrylyshyn 1995). The Havrylyshyn (1995 p. 4) report reiterates the common belief that although the speed of reform, its sequencing, and political integration is debated, "the actions that bring PCEs to an economy that is largely privately owned, with free and open markets, in a predominately competitive environment, and broadly open to global markets," create little controversy. Groupings based on the economic or political variables which bring the countries closest to this ideal, suggest groupings of countries which have similar marketing environments.

Likewise, trade alliances and coalitions are especially important for economic growth and clusters based on membership might also be useful for marketing practitioners. The authors have also used cluster analysis of countries, based on country membership in 31 economic organizations, which show sub-groups similar to the IMF groupings.

Others have argued that foreign investment in the region will be the most powerful catalyst for economic and political change (e.g., Sokhin 1994; Meth-Cohn et al. 1994; and Donges and Wieners 1992). Factor analysis of investors' perceptions of foreign investment again show similar groupings. Interestingly, despite using a number of variables and methods, only a few countries defy traditional geo-cultural groupings (Baltics, Central Europe, Eastern Europe, Russia and Orthodox peripheral, and Central Asia). Most of those not consistently fitting into clusters are the countries of the former Yugoslavia and Albania for which data is not always available.

Regardless of the method used to group the countries together, clear sub-constructs appear. Similar multivariate interdependence analyses, encompassing a greater range of phenomena will undoubtedly reveal other, probably similar sub-groupings. The accumulation of such data would allow a more precise and reliable constitutive definition of the East European construct and aid in explaining and predicting phenomena in the region. For the moment, the authors suggest discarding the term 'Eastern Europe' in favor of more precise sub-groupings. If the term is to encompass all the countries of the region, the authors suggest the term "post command economies," which is all encompassing and has a political/economic, rather than a cultural delineation.

METHODOLOGICAL CONCERNS WITH REGIONAL RESEARCH

Despite ethnocentrism (and its inherent dangers) being a well-established concept taught at all levels of international business, it is probably fair to say that most of the comparative research carried out in the PCEs by Western organizations has been conducted from a Western viewpoint and, therefore, it is likely to be biased and culturally bound. Even for studies which are not primarily comparative in nature, their evaluative measures are overwhelmingly of Western origin.

This is not to say such research is inherently fatal (Irwin et al. 1977). Imposed measurements may be appropriate where the investigator is interested in predicting behavior or identifying perceptions on a specific criterion which is exported from the Western culture. For example, the effectiveness of package or advertising campaign may use the same measures to determine the likely success of the same campaign. Research also suggests (Naroll 1970) that cultural diffusion takes place among groups in contact with each other. Predicting managerial or consumer behavior may, indeed, be appropriate given the amount of training programs, education, technological assistance and marketing strategies that are being exported from the West. Similarly some have argued that it is legitimate to make such comparisons when cultures are striving towards Western technology (Vernon 1969). In fact, there is a good deal of research that points to world-wide harmonization of phenomena (Firat 1995; Levitt 1983; Paddison et al. 1990; Knox and Agnew 1989; Goodman and Michael 1990) and in the case of many PCEs, concerted effort toward membership in Western communities. If this is so, the use of Western measures in the region may be appropriate.

Other researchers have argued that the Western experiences may not apply in the region (e.g., Savitt 1994; Kadar 1991). Such researchers contend that "the rules of the game may be different and the theories explaining developed market economies are not valid or only valid to a limited extent" (Kadar 1991). We cannot, therefore, assume that successful models developed in other countries can be readily applied to the region (Greer 1995).

Culturally biased studies are understandable given the nature of most PCE research. Most Western aid organizations that commission studies (e.g., EC, OECD, EBRD, etc.) hire Western firms or consultants to carry out the studies. This stems, in part, to the initial lack of indigenous management and marketing research expertise in the region and, in particular, to the lack of experience in consumer-based research. It has been suggested, however, that the use of Western researchers and consultants is

FIGURE 1. Country Groupings

Pre-1990 Groupings	IMF (1995) Groupings Based on status of free market reforms)[1,2]	Trade Association Membership (Cluster Analyisis)[1]
Eastern Europe Poland Czechoslovakia East Germany Hungary Bulgaria Romania **Soviet Union** Latvia Lithuania Estonia Belarus Georgia Ukraine Russia Moldova Armenia Kyrgizia Azerbaijan Kazakhstan Taijkistan Turkmenistan Uzbekistan **Yugoslavia** Croatia Macedonia Slovenia Bosnia Serbia **Other Communist** Albania	**IMF-Group 1a** Albania Czech Republic Poland Slovenia **IMF-Group 1b** Croatia Estonia Latvia Lithuania **IMF-Group 2** Bulgaria Hungary Romania Slovakia **IMF-Group 3** Armenia Georgia Kazakhstan Kyrgyz Republic Moldova Russia Ukraine Macedonia **IMF-Group 4** Azerbaijan Belarus Tajikistan Turkmenistan Uzbekistan	**Cluster 1** Poland Czech Republic Slovakia Hungary Bulgaria Romania Lithuania Latvia Estonia **Cluster 2** Belarus Georgia Ukraine Russia Moldova Armenia **Cluster 3** Azerbaijan Kyrgyz Republic Kazakhstan Tajikistan Turkmenistan Uzbekistan **Cluster 4** Albania Macedonia Slovenia

(1) Not all nations are included in each analysis
(2) IMF 1a = early reformers, first wave, succeeding; IMF 1b = early reformers, second wave, succeeding; IMF 2 = early reformers, stalling; IMF 3 = lagging reformers, substantial start; IMF 4 = lagging reformers, limited start

Foreign Investment Risk (Factor Analysis)[1]	Geo-Cultural Groupings
Factor 1 Czech Republic Poland Slovakia Hungary	**Central Europe** Czech Republic Poland Slovakia Hungary Slovenia
Factor 2 Bulgaria Romania Moldova Croatia Macedonia Georgia	**Eastern Europe** Bulgaria Romania Moldova Croatia Macedonia Serbia Bosnia Albania
Factor 3 Albania Armenia Russia Ukraine	**Russia & Peripheral** Russia Ukraine Belarus Georgia Armenia
Factor 4 Belarus Lithuania Latvia Estonia Kazakhstan	**Baltics** Lithuania Latvia Estonia
Factor 5 Azerbaijan Kyrgyz Republic Tajikistan Turkmenistan Uzbekistan	**Central Asia** Kazakhstan Azerbaijan Kyrgyz Republic Tajikistan Turkmenistan Uzbekistan

more reflective of the desire for Western aid to be recycled back into the West via the accounts of Western consultants (see Foster 1993).

Another problem, addressed by Berrien (1967) and Altheide and Johnson (1994) relates to the consciously or unconsciously writing up of phenomena in terms familiar to the Western readers' (writers') pattern of life or thought. Because a person's thought framework is inevitably anchored in his/her own culture, interpretations (both in the writing and reading of PCE phenomena) are likely to be ethnocentric. Studies can be made more meaningful and less ethnocentric by explaining the context (the setting and situation) of the research, reporting multiplicity of meanings and perspectives, and the rationality of these perspectives (Altheide and Johnson 1994).

Pike (1965) and Berry (1969; 1979; 1989) have coined the terms *emic* and *etic* to describe two different standpoints from which to describe cross-cultural phenomena. Their work is particularly useful in that it contributes to our understanding of the dangers inherent in assuming phenomena are universal. Their methodology also assists in deciding research approaches and interpreting research results. The etic viewpoint (derived from the word "phonetic") is studying from outside a particular system while the emic viewpoint (derived from the word "phonemic") results from studying behavior from inside the system. According to Berry (1969) emics apply only in a particular society while etics are culture-free or universal aspects of the world (or at least operate in more than one society). Pike stresses that both approaches are valuable and neither is more important than the other. Neither do the viewpoints form a dichotomy. In fact, Berry (1969 p. 123) stresses the need to "describe behavior in terms which are meaningful to members of a particular culture (emic approach) and at the same time validly compare behavior in that culture with behavior in another or all other cultures (etic approach)."

When principles or phenomena are simply assumed to be common across cultures (universal), without theoretical or empirical evidence, the universals are said to have been "imposed" (Berry 1969) or are "pseudo-etics" (Triandis et al. 1971). As Berry (1972 p. 12) points out, a great many of these pseudo-etics are simply "Euro-American emics imposed on phenomena in other cultures." If the cost and effort of gathering PCE data that is ineffectual is to be avoided, researchers must operationalise imposed research measures (imposed etics).

In 1989, Berry devised five steps that can be operationalised to increase the reliability and validity of cross-cultural research (see Figure 2). In step 1 the researcher develops a concept and tests as in the normal research process. Step 2 is then taken with the same test in another culture; at most there is linguistic translation and maybe even some cultural translation. It is at this step, the imposed etic, that many people researching PCEs have stopped.

In step 3 there is a deliberate attempt to come to know and assess the other culture as reliably and as validly as one knows one's own (as in step 1). This requires the use of ethnographic or psychometric techniques. In step 4, the two emic understandings are compared to each other. If no commonalities exist, whether conceptually or empirically, than a comparison is simply not possible. Step 5 is when the researcher decides whether sufficient commonality exists to make a comparison. If there is enough commonality, the researcher uses a 'derived etic.' As Irwin et al. (1977) note, measures are derived etic only if they have grown out of both etic and emic analyses which means being heavily dependent on local informants for guidance.

The idea that measures used in cross-cultural studies must be equivalent in order to be meaningfully compared has been discussed in detail by many others (e.g., Douglas et al. 1994; Goldschmidt 1966; Frijda and Johoda 1966). Establishing equivalence is not, however, an easy task. Berry and Dasen (1975) suggest three kinds of equivalence exist: functional, conceptual and metric.

Functional equivalence exists when similar activities have similar functions. To illustrate functional equivalence it is useful to look at the functional equivalence of management in the PCEs and the West (Table 2). Kenny and Trick (1995) found that the separation of managerial functions and lack of any relationship between price, quality, and cost meant PCE managers had no current knowledge of sales or profitability of a system which was clearly divergent from managers in a free market system. (Indigenous PCE experiences [e.g., Kaniskin 1991] have reported similar problems with functional equivalence.) Noar (1994) similarly notes that environmental conditions in PCEs require differing managerial approaches and differing applications of principles and concepts, whether in marketing or in other business disciplines. Given these conditions, to make a direct comparison of, for example, management efficiency or effectiveness, might be inappropriate.

Others have also struggled with comparing PCE management with the West (Luthans et al. 1993; Graham et al. 1992; Reynolds and Young 1992; Hermann 1992, etc.). Many have utilized the ethnographic technique, though its practice, in some cases, is somewhat underdeveloped. Most, however, recognized the fundamental need to understand the role and function of management in this different type of culture. Reynolds and Young (1992) came to the conclusion that it is necessary to have a foundation of practical experience with the people and organization before com-

FIGURE 2. Cross-Cultural Research Approaches Applied to PCE Phenomena

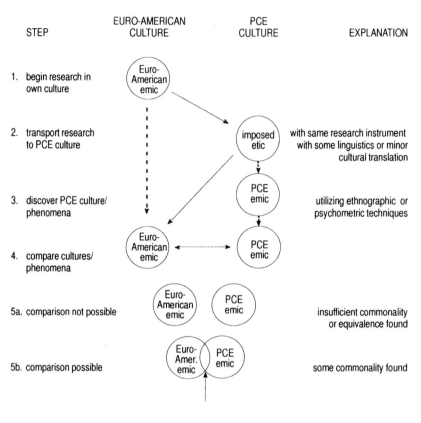

| | EURO-AMERICAN | PCE | |
| STEP | CULTURE | CULTURE | EXPLANATION |

1. begin research in own culture — Euro-American emic

2. transport research to PCE culture — imposed etic — with same research instrument with some linguistics or minor cultural translation

3. discover PCE culture/ phenomena — PCE emic — utilizing ethnographic or psychometric techniques

4. compare cultures/ phenomena — Euro-American emic ↔ PCE emic

5a. comparison not possible — Euro-American emic / PCE emic — insufficient commonality or equivalence found

5b. comparison possible — Euro-Amer. emic / PCE emic — some commonality found

derived etic

Source: derived from Berry, J.W. (1989).

TABLE 2. Functional Inequivalence of Management

West (Free Market) System	Command System
meeting demand	meeting quotas
growth, synergy, integration often horizontal	non-profit
unbundling and asset stripping	assets difficult to value

Source: Kenny and Trick 1995.

parisons can be made. Hermann (1992) also stressed the difficulty faced by Western business people and academics in terms of having a mutual understanding of fundamental concepts with their counterparts in a PCE. These are common problems ethnographers face.

A concern with the ethnographic approach to cross-cultural comparisons is that it poses problematic issues with regard to validity because of its potential for subjectivity. Furthermore, ethnography is best used: to explore phenomena rather than test phenomena; when data is unstructured; when there is only one or a few cases under investigation; and when verbal descriptions will take a subordinate role to quantification or statistical analysis (Atkinson and Hammersley 1994). To increase validity of ethnographic research, Altheide and Johnson (1994) suggest that the process must be clearly delineated, including accounts of the interactions among context, researcher, method, setting and actors. Nader (1993) suggests that true ethnography entails deep immersion and is seldom accomplished in short periods of time (a criteria most PCE research fails). Another key part of the ethnographic method is to see first hand what occurs; failing that, ethnographers would ask informants and others for their recollections, points of view, and interpretations (Altheide and Johnson 1994). It is vital that researchers investigating PCE phenomena consider and report on these points, so that readers can assess the validity of qualitative results.

Conceptual equivalence implies that the meaning of research materials (stimuli, concepts, etc.) are the same. At the basic level this means that measures and criteria must be translated correctly. To combat problems with conceptual equivalence, researchers could use a variety of techniques, including back translation of words and sentences, bilingual translation, or committee translation (Brislin 1970). Researchers should also be aware, however, that even if such translation techniques are used, concepts may still be misinterpreted. Cui-chi (1995) suggests considering *isomorphic* equivalency since most phenomena are based on self-reference criteria. This self-reference criteria manifests itself in the language of a population and may alter the connotative meaning in an etymological sense. For example, the concept of "supermarket" was found to be divergent in the PCEs and Western cultures. For Westerners, the term supermarket means having self-service, high volume/low cost sales and sales floor area in excess of $1000m^2$. When exploring food shopping behavior in Bulgaria, over 90 percent of the respondents stated they used supermarkets despite statistical figures showing just two supermarkets in existence (Mueller 1994). Delhaize (1993) noted similar discrepancies in Hungary, where almost all shops, regardless of size or format, were termed "supermarket."

Another problem researchers encounter is different statistical measures which are often employed. For instance, while many western countries record statistics based on the Standard Industrial Code (SIC), the post command economies did not. Similarly, the PCEs used Net Material Product (NMP) rather than Gross Domestic or National Product (GDP or GNP) to measure economic output. Translation of one to the other is a highly subjective exercise, making historical comparisons extremely unreliable.

A less salient problem with conceptual equivalence, especially in cross-cultural studies, is related to spatial distances in scale measurements. Researchers should recognize that cultural idiosyncrasies may play a part in the use of scale range. Baron and Mueller (1995) have noted that some PCE respondents tend to be more emphatic, making substantial use of the extreme ends of the measurement scales. Researchers should be aware that such biases might exist and that these could affect the validity of straight comparison of means.

Metric equivalence exists when the psychometric properties of two or more sets of data or observations from two or more cultural groups exhibit essentially the same coherence or structure. Unlike functional or conceptual equivalence, metric equivalence can only be established after the data have been collected and analyzed (Berry 1994). Many PCE researchers have not attempted to adequately determine the necessary prerequisites of cross-cultural commonalities with respect to the invariance (comparability) of their constructs.

A lot of marketing research requires operating in the realm of constructs that cannot be measured directly; constructs must be operationalised or linked to behavior that can be measured. Consequently, much perceptual and behavioral research makes use of psychometric procedures. In cross-cultural studies, the factor analytic approach is probably the most potent procedure available for determining the cross-cultural validity of psychological constructs (Buss and Royce 1975).

Prior to the mid-1980s, the method most often used for determining psychometric equivalence was exploratory factor analysis, yet determining the invariance of factor structures with this method was highly subjective. The development of confirmatory factor analysis models (Joreskog and Sorbom 1984), however, have made comparing country or cross-cultural data rather straightforward. This can be done by collecting similar data in each culture or by collecting data in one culture and retesting it against the factor model established in other cultures (Watkins 1989; Durvasula et al. 1993). Another advantage of confirmatory factor analysis is that it allows researchers to probe dimensions within a construct. By probing the dimensions of a construct, the researcher may be able to devise an interpretable representation of the construct's validity and meaning in the host country and its overlap with constructs emic to his own culture (Irwin et al. 1977).

Though Watkins (1989) suggests problems with the availability, expense and difficulty of using confirmatory factor analysis are decreasing, it is still relatively expensive and difficult to employ researchers without organizational support. The oldest and probably most widely used package, SPSS LISREL (sold as an add-on to the SPSS program) does not appear to be widely used outside the United States. Its use is not taught in most business courses and although there are a number of 'user friendly' guides, researchers without strong statistical backgrounds may find it intimidating (Diamantopolis 1994). Nevertheless, confirmatory factor analysis models offer cross-cultural market researchers the best mechanism for testing psychometric equivalence of constructs across cultures.

CONCLUSION

The opening of the post command economies is exciting. Not only does the region offer organizations tremendous market potential but it offers marketing academics the opportunity to test new or existing hypotheses under distinctly different situations. There is, however, sufficient debate as to whether there is any commonality between Western economies and the PCEs or even commonality among PCEs. These two issues merit serious attention.

In the rush to explore phenomena in PCEs, many marketing researchers and consultants have failed to consider fundamental issues of cross-cultural inquiry. Those who derive their expertise based on Western theory and practice should, at the very least, entertain the notion that what may hold true in Western cultures may not in the PCEs. This is especially true in the PCE region as there is no precedence of countries leaving a command system and embarking on a free market one; experts' knowledge and experience is necessarily limited.

Yet there is a need to explore and understand what is happening in the PCE market so that firms, governments, and individuals can make choices and predictions. When examining phenomena in the PCEs, marketers can learn much from anthropologists, linguists, sociologists and cross-cultural psychologists who have been instrumental in developing appropriate methods for the operationalising of cross-cultural methods and practice. By considering scientific methods developed by these researchers, marketing theorists and practitioners can design better programs which increase the validity or research results and effectiveness of marketing programs in the PCEs.

Because of the rise in national cultures, coupled with political and economic autonomy, individual national studies are recommended. It is recognized, however, that individual PCEs are often too small for firms to gain sufficient leverage with marketing programs and strategies; it is often necessary to create larger sub-groups. The use of multivariate interdependence techniques such as factor and cluster analyses are tools marketers can use to create more viable PCE sub-groups. That these procedures have been used by the authors and others and show political and economic sub-groupings similar to the traditional geo-cultural groupings suggests that more appropriate and useful PCE sub-groupings are already in existence.

Finally, it has been over five years since the collapse of the command system. In the immediate aftermath, exploratory research methods were necessary to help aid our understanding of business phenomena in PCEs. It is time to move on to more rigorous analyses and hypotheses testing. In particular, the authors recommend the use of more sophisticated multivariate statistical techniques to test hypotheses developed using qualitative methods. Confirmatory factor analysis, for example, can aid in determining whether marketing constructs are universal (or common across nations). This kind of information can be useful for managers in deciding whether to implement multi-national (or global) marketing strategies.

NOTES

1. An earlier version of this paper was presented at the Conference on Central and Eastern Europe: 5 Years On, 20-21 June 1995, Buckinghamshire College (Brunel University), Buckinghamshire, England. The authors acknowledge their grateful appreciation for participants' thoughts and suggestions which have been incorporated into this revised edition.

2. Council for Mutual Economic Assistance (now defunct) included: Bulgaria, Hungary, Poland, Czechoslovakia, USSR, Albania, East Germany, Mongolia, Cuba. Romania, Vietnam and Yugoslavia (associate).

REFERENCES

Altheide, D. and Johnson, J. (1994). Criteria for Assessing Interpretive Validity in Qualitative Research. In Denzin, N. and Lincoln, S. (Eds.) *Handbook of Qualitative Research* (pp. 485-499). Thousand Oaks: Sage Publications.

Anon. (1995). *Global Politics in the 1990s*. Brochure for Examining the Impact of the End of the Cold War on Teaching and Research Faculty Symposium, Cincinnati World Affairs Council, Cincinnati (September 14-16).

Applebaum, A. (1994). The Real Danger in Eastern Europe. *The Wall Street Journal* (November 28th).

Atkinson, P. and Hammersley, M. (1994). Ethnography and Participant Observation. In Denzin, N. and Lincoln, S. (Eds.) *Handbook of Qualitative Research* (pp. 248-261). Thousand Oaks: Sage Publications.

Baeva, I. (1991). Eastern Europe Past and Present. *Bulgarian Quarterly Review* (March), 33-43.

Baron, P. and Mueller, R. (1995). Consumer Expectations in Eastern European Food Markets. *British Food Journal*, 97(2), 34-38.

Berrien, F. K. (1967). Methodological and Related Problems in Cross-cultural. *Research International Journal of Psychology*, 2(1), 33-43.

Berry, J. W. (1969). On Cross-cultural Comparability. *International Journal of Psychology*, 4, 119-128.

Berry, J. W. (1979). Research in Multi-cultural Societies Implications of Cross-cultural Methods. *Journal of Cross-cultural Psychology*, 10(4), 415-434..

Berry, J. W. (1972). Introduction to Methodology. In Triandis, H. and Berry, J. W. (Eds.) *Handbook of Cross-cultural Psychology* (pp. 1-28). Boston: Allyn and Bacon.

Berry, J. W. (1989). Imposed Etics-Emic-Derived Etics: The Operationalisation of a Compelling Idea. *International Journal of Psychology*, 24, 721-735.

Berry, J. W. (1994). Methodological Concerns. In Berry, J. W., Poortinga, Y., Segall, M., and Dasen, P. (Eds.) *Cross-cultural Psychology: Research and Applications* Cambridge: University Press.

Berry, J. W., Poortinga, Y., Segall, M., and Dasen, P. (Eds.) (1994). *Cross-cultural Psychology: Research and Applications*. Cambridge: University Press.

Berry, J. W. and Dasen, P. (1975). *Culture and Cognition*. London: Methuen.

Brislin, R. (1970). Back-translation for Cross-cultural Research. *Journal of Cross-cultural Psychology*, 1, 185-216.

Burr, B. (1993). Ethnic Cries Could Spread to Portfolios, *Pensions and Investments*, 23, 14-12.

Business Eastern Europe (1993). Getting the Statistics Right. *East European Statistics*, XXII (6), April 19.

Buss, A. and Royce, J. (1975). Detecting Cross-cultural Commonalities and Differences: Intergroup Factor Analysis. *Psychological Bulletin*, 28(1), 129-136.

Costa, J. and Bamossy, G. (1995). *Marketing in a Multi-cultural World*. Thousand Oaks: Sage Publications.

Cui-chi, C. (1995). Managerial Role Expectations in Sino-British Joint Ventures: Match or Mismatch? *Leicester Business School Occasional Paper 28*, Leicester England: De Montfort University.

Diamantopolis, A. (1994). Modelling with LISREAL: A Guide for the Uninitiated. In Hooley, G. and Hussey, M. (Eds.), *Quantitative Methods in Marketing* (pp. 103-136). London: Academic Press.

Delhaize, P. (1993). Future Relations Between the European Community and Hungary. Paper presented at Club Bruxelles Conference (December), Brussels.

Donges, L., and Wieners, K. (1992). Foreign Investment in Eastern Europe's Transformation and Process. Paper presented at International Study Group Conference on Investment, University of Nottingham, England (September 11-13).

Douglas, S., Morrin, M., and Craig, S. (1994). Cross-national Consumer Research Traditions. In Laurent, G., Lillien, G., and Pras, B. (Eds.) *Research Traditions in Marketing* (pp. 51-69). Boston: Kluwer Academic.

Durvasula, S., Andrews, J., Lysonski, S., and Netemeyer, R. (1993). Assessing the Cross-national Applicability of Consumer Behavior Models: A Model of Attitude toward Advertising in General. *Journal of International Business Studies*, 19 (March), 626-636.

Firat, A. (1995). Consumer Culture or Culture Consumed. In Costa, J. and Bamossy, G. *Marketing in a Multi-cultural World*. Thousand Oaks: Sage Publications.

Foster, A. (1993). Capitalism Goes East. *Eurobusiness* (May), 8-18.

Frijda, N. and Johoda, G. (1966). On the Scope and Methods of Cross-cultural Research. *International Psychology*, 11(1), 109-127.

Goldschmidt, W. (1966). *Comparative Functionalism*. Berkeley, CA: University of California Press.

Goodman, D. and Michael, R. (1990). The Farm Crisis and the Food System: Some Reflections on the New Agenda. *Political, Social and Economic Perspective on the International Food System*. Averbury: Gower Publishing Limited, 19-35.

Graham, J., Evenko, L., and Rajan., M. (1992). An Empirical Comparison of Soviet and American Business Negotiations. *Journal of International Business Studies*, 3rd Quarter, 387-418.

Greer, W. (1995). Management Education Reforms in the Baltic States: Preliminary Observations. *Journal of East-West Business*, 1 (1).

Havrylyshyn, O. (1995). Economic Transformation: The Tasks Still Ahead. Paper presented at The Per Jacobsson Symposium (October).

Hermann, M. (1992). *Management Training During the Process of Transition from a Command to Market Economy*. Paper presented at the AMEDC Conference on Management Development Needs in Central Eastern Europe, London Business School (November 5).

Irwin, M., Klein, R., Engle, P., Yarborough, C. and Nerlove (1977). The Problem of Establishing Validity in Cross-cultural Measurements. *Research Annals New York Academy of Sciences*, 308-325.

Jeannet, J-P. and Hennessey, H. (1992). *Global Marketing Strategies*. Boston: Houghton Miffin Company.

Joreskog, K. and Sorbom, D. (1984). *LISREL VI: User's Guide*. Mooresville, Ind: Scientific Software Inc.

Kadar, B. (1991). Central Europe Once Again. *The New Hungarian Quarterly*, 21(32), 3-18.

Kaniskin, N.A. (1991). The Western Manager and the Soviet Director. *The Soviet Review*, (May-June), 41-51.

Kenny, B. and Trick, B. (1995). Reform and Management Education: A Case from the Czech Republic. *Journal of East-West Business*, 1(1), 69-95.

Knox, P. and Agnew, J. (1989). *The Geography of the World*. London: Routledge, Chapmans and Hall.

Levitt, T. (1983). The Globalisation of Markets. *Harvard Business Review* (May/June).

Luthans, F., Welsh, D., and Rosenkrantz, S. (1993). What Do Russian Managers Really Do? An Observational Study with Comparisons to U.S. Managers. *Journal of International Business Studies*, 4th Quarter, 741-761.

Marks, J. (1994, January 10). Remembrance of things past: renascent nationalism titillates Central Europe's Intellectual Circles. *U.S. New and World Report*, pp. 28-35.

McDaniel, C. and Gates, R. (1993). *Contemporary Marketing Research*. London: West Publishing.

Mellor, R. (1975). *Eastern Europe: A Geography of Comecon*. London: McMillian.

Meth-Cohn, D., Kasriel, K., Klopf, P., Komlev, S., Simpson, P., and Torniley, D. (1994, April). The Engine of Growth: Foreign Investors are Changing Their Tactics for Moving into Central and Eastern Europe. *Business Central Europe*, pp. 35-50.

Mueller, R. (1994). Food Distribution Efficiency in Eastern Europe. Unpublished PhD Thesis. Leicester, England: De Montfort University.

Nader, L. (1993). Paradigm Busting and Vertical Linkages. *Contemporary Psychology*, 33, 6-7.

Naroll, R. (1970). Galton's Problem. In Naroll, R. and Cohen, R. (Eds.) *Handbook of Method and Cultural Anthropology*, New York: Natural History Press.

Noar, J. (1994). Marketing Under Newly-emerging East European and Soviet Conditions–Some Thoughts on What Needs to be Done. *The Economics of Change in East and Central Europe*. London: Academic Press, 343-353.

Paddison, R., Findlay, A., and Dawson, J. (1990). Retailing in Lesser Developed Countries. *The Theory and Practice of Retail Studies*. New York: Routledge.

Pike, K. (1965). *The Language in Relation to a Unified Theory of the Structure of Human Behavior*. The Hague: Mouton.

Pribova, M. (1993). *Evolving Values in Eastern Europe Celakovice*. Czech Republic: Czechoslovak Management Center.

Reynolds, P. and Young, P. (1992). *Eastern Promise: Privatization Strategy for Post-communist Countries*. Adam Smith Institute.

Savitt, R. (1994). Comment: The Evolution of Distribution Systems. *International Marketing Review*, 11(2):47-51.

Sokhin, A. (1994). Foreign Economic Activity in Russian Investment. *Opportunities in The Former Soviet Union*, 9-16.

Staede, R. D. (1978). Multinational Corporations and the Changing World Economic Order. *California Management Review* (Winter), 7.

Terry, S. M.(1993). Comment: Thinking about post-communist transitions: how different are they? *Slavic Review* (Summer), 333-337.

Triandis, H. C., R. S. Malpass and A. Davidson (1971). Cross-cultural psychology. Biennial Review of Anthropology. 1-84.

Vernon, P. (1969). Intelligence and Cultural Environment. London: Metheun.

Waltzer, M. (1994, September 11). Between Nation and World. *The Economist*, 328,7828, pp. 49-52.

Watkins, D. (1989). The Role of Confirmatory Factor Analysis in Cross-cultural Research. *International Journal of Psychology*, 24, 685-701.

Environmental Dimensions of Emerging Markets: Introducing a Region-Relevant Market Analysis Matrix

Dana-Nicoleta Lascu
Lalita A. Manrai
Ajay K. Manrai

SUMMARY. This paper offers an alternative classification/clustering of the countries in Central and Eastern Europe on the dimensions of marketization and Westernization. It argues that these dimensions are more useful to marketing analysts and other marketing practitioners in their attempt to understand the complex markets of Central and Eastern Europe, since they are more focused and directly relevant to the practice of marketing, compared to the broader dimensions most often used to define marketing developments in the region: economic development and culture. *[Article copies available for a*

Dana-Nicoleta Lascu is Assistant Professor of marketing at the University of Richmond. She teaches global marketing and marketing management.

Lalita A. Manrai is Associate Professor of marketing at the University of Delaware. She teaches global marketing and marketing management.

Ajay K. Manrai is an Associate Professor of marketing at the University of Delaware. He teaches marketing research and marketing management.

The authors would like to express their gratitude to the anonymous reviewers for their comments and suggestions on the manuscript.

[Haworth co-indexing entry note]: "Environmental Dimensions of Emerging Markets: Introducing a Region-Relevant Market Analysis Matrix." Lascu, Dana-Nicoleta, Lalita A. Manrai, and Ajay K. Manrai. Co-published simultaneously in *Journal of East-West Business* (International Business Press, an imprint of The Haworth Press, Inc.) Vol. 3, No. 1, 1996, pp. 27-41; and: *Marketing in Central and Eastern Europe* (ed: Jan Nowak) International Business Press, an imprint of The Haworth Press, Inc., 1996, pp. 27-41. Single or multiple copies of this article are available for a fee from The Haworth Document Delivery Service [1-800-342-9678, 9:00 a.m. - 5:00 p.m. (EST). E-mail address: getinfo@haworth.com].

27

INTRODUCTION

Central and Eastern Europe may, on the surface, appear to be a homogeneous market, a market where consumers have similar backgrounds (Slavic origin, Catholic and Eastern Orthodox religion being unifying characteristics) and preferences—mostly for Western goods—while lacking the wherewithal to purchase these same goods. This picture is misleading, since there are substantial differences between these countries that must be noted by marketing practitioners planning an engagement in this region. When market analysts do note differences between the countries of Central and Eastern Europe, it is in terms of the level of economic development (standard of living, buying power) of the various countries, or relative to the cultural characteristics that are shared in different sub-regions—differences pertaining to origin, language, and religion, among others.

The purpose of this study is to suggest two differentiation dimensions which could provide additional utility to marketing practitioners planning to have a presence in these countries, and, hopefully, a better understanding of market developments in the region. One of the dimensions is the countries' level of Westernization, defined here as the countries' proximity to the West and the duration and extent of their openness to Western influence, cultural or otherwise. The Westernization dimension draws on a number of factors: proximity to the West, travel permitted in the past decades, as well as century-long traditions of relations with Western countries; for instance, Hungary's ties to Austria, Slovenia's ties to Italy.

The other dimension is marketization, defined in the marketing literature as the extent to which countries experience dramatic exposure to global communications, dramatic increases in the availability of foreign as well as domestic products . . . an overall attempt by society, which feels that it has missed out on something, to quickly close the gap between them and the more developed countries (cf. Ger, Belk and Lascu 1993, p. 106). Marketization reflects a set of institutional and cultural requirements for the operation of effective private markets, such as materialistic values as a stimulus for greater production, efficient forms of competition, freedom of information, honesty in government, security of persons and property, deferring gratification to generate private savings, and rationality unconstrained by tradition (Keyfitz and Dorfan 1991). The study proposes to identify country clusters in Central and Eastern Europe that are defined in terms of Westernization and marketization, clusters which may cut across decades-old national boundaries.[1]

In the next section, the paper will address the factors typically used by marketing analysts and other marketing practitioners to differentiate between the countries in the region: culture and, more recently, level of economic development. In the background section, the authors will argue for a classification/clustering approach that is more meaningful and useful for marketing practitioners, using Westernization and marketization as the key dimensions.

BACKGROUND

One factor that is sometimes used in distinguishing between the different countries of Central and Eastern Europe is culture. Culture is defined as the accumulation and learning of shared meanings, rituals, norms and traditions among the members of a society (Solomon 1996). Culture and marketing are intricately linked, given that much of the behavior of consumers, as well as that of marketing managers, researchers, salespeople, etc., is determined by their cultural background–culture is a fundamental determinant of a person's wants and behavior. In marketing terms, culture includes abstract ideas, such as values and ethics, as well as the material objects and services produced or valued by a society, such as clothing, food, shelter, etc., in the different forms they take in various countries.

Central and Eastern European countries have been categorized based on the different factors: origin, language, and religion. Other components of culture, such as education and social organizations (Solomon 1996) are, more often than not, shared by the countries in the region–high level of education, nuclear family, concern with status and status reversal (Lascu, Manrai and Manrai 1994a). These different factors, then, are not helpful in differentiating between the countries of Mitteleuropa and Eastern Europe.

Origins and Language

One method of categorizing the countries of Central and Eastern Europe is on the basis of origin and religion. The only people that can be traced to this area beyond 2,000 years are Romanians. Romanians come from the Dacian tribes that have been documented to inhabit the Eastern Carpathian mountains since the year 2,000 before the current era. These tribes were then assimilated at the beginning of the first millennium by the Romans, who established there one of the most important legions. Consequently, Romanians are the only Eastern European people to have a Roman heritage and speak a Romance language.

Hungary also has a unique background to the region: its people belonged to the Hun tribes, originating in Asia. The language they speak is Hungarian, part of the Finno-Ugric family of languages. Most of the remaining countries in Central and Eastern Europe trace their roots to the Slav tribes, which also originate in Asia. The languages–Czech, Slovak, Slovene, Serbian, Bulgarian, Polish, Russian, etc.–are all of Slavic origin and have much in common. Thus, three main language families exist in Central and Eastern Europe: Slavic, Romance, and Finno-Ugric.

It should be noted that languages other than national languages are spoken in these countries. It is important to note specifically which are the commercial languages spoken in the respective countries, since these are the languages that may be used by marketing practitioners. Table 1 lists the commercial languages used in the different countries in Central and Eastern Europe. Note that German is a frequently used language of trade, especially in the countries situated in the more central region of Europe, while Russian is frequently used as a language for business in the countries with a Slavic ancestry. Other languages reflect the existence of extended ties to certain cultures: for instance, in Albania, Italian is still widely spoken, and, in Romania, French is also frequently encountered, proof of enduring ties with the respective cultures (see Table 1).

Religion

The dominant religions in the area are Catholic and the so-called "Eastern rite of the Catholic church"–Eastern Orthodox. The countries that are predominantly Catholic are the Czech Republic, Hungary, Poland, and Slovakia. Countries that are predominantly Eastern Orthodox are Bulgaria, Romania, Serbia, Slovenia, and Croatia (see Table 2), as well as most of

TABLE 1. Commercial Languages Spoken in Central and Eastern Europe

Country	Commercial Language(s)
Albania	Albanian, French, Italian
Bulgaria	Bulgarian, English, Russian
The Czech Republic	Czech, Slovak, English, German
Hungary	Hungarian, German, English, Russian
Poland	Polish, German, English
Romania	Romanian, French, English, German
Serbia	Serb, English, German, Russian
Slovakia	Slovak, Czech, English
Slovenia	Slovene, English, German, Russian

TABLE 2. Country Profiles for Central and Eastern Europe

	Albania	Bulgaria	Czech Republic	Slovakia	Hungary	Poland	Romania
Populations (Millions)	3.2	9.3	10.5	5.3	10.7	38.3	23.5
Urban	35.7%	67.9%	77.5%	77.5%	60.9%	62%	52.7%
Ethnic Groups	Albanian 90% Greek 8%	Bulgarian 83.5% Turkish 8.5% Romany 2.6% Macedonia 2.5%	Czech 95%	Slovak 86% Hungarian 11%	Hungarian 92% Romany 3%	Polish 99%	Romanian 89% Hungarian 7.9% Germany 1.6%
Religion	Muslim 70% Eastern Orthodox 20% Catholic 10%	Eastern Orthodox Catholic	Catholic Protestant	Catholic 60% Protestant	Catholic 68% Calvinist 20% Lutheran 5%	Catholic 95%	Eastern Orthodox 80% Catholic 6%
Form of Government	Legislative People's Assembly	Parliamentary Republic	Parliamentary Republic	Parliamentary Republic	Parliamentary Democracy	Democratic Union	Parliamentary Republic
GDP Per Capita (in dollars)		3,669	3,000	1,900	3,200	1,678	1,618
GNP Per Capita (in dollars)	1,200	1,853				1,800	1,618
Imports Per Capita (in dollars)					816	408	392
Exports Per Capita (in dollars)					900	392	253
Per Capita Consumer Expenditure (in dollars)	967	577			1,848	1,472	1,176
Imports from/Exports to Germany EC EFTA CMEA		21.9%/10.5% 39.4%/30.1% 7.1%/4.6% 16 %/23.4%	(Former Czechoslovakia) 21.0%/17.9% 31.1%/32.0% 15.4%/10.7% 16.4%/11.8%		17.4%/17.1% 30.9%/32.4% 15.3%/12.0% 27.9%/28.3%	26.5%/18.3% 45.0%/35.7% 10.1/8.7% 27.9%/37.1%	11.4%/11.0% 19.6%/31.4% 4.0%/3.6% 35.9%/34.7%

Sources: Euromonitor 1995, Euromonitor 1993, Country Profiles 1995.

the newly-independent European republics of the former Soviet Union. Other religions are also prominent in the region: Protestant religions constitute a significant minority in Hungary, where 20% of the population are Calvinist and 5% are Lutheran, but are also present in Central Europe (the Czech Republic, Slovakia), as well as in Transylvania–the region of Romania that has been under the Austro-Hungarian empire and has consequently benefitted from significant Western cultural influence, relative to Moldova and Wallachia, the other main regions of Romania.

There is also a significant Muslim presence in many countries of Central and Eastern Europe,[2] originating from the region's history of dominance by the Turkish empire; in fact, Albania has a large majority of Muslims–70% (see Table 2). Typically, the Muslim populations face discrimination and annihilation attempts, as evidenced by the crises in the former Yugoslavia.

ECONOMIC DEVELOPMENT: A MACRO PERSPECTIVE

A more frequently-used approach to clustering the countries of Central and Eastern Europe is based on economic development. Central and Eastern Europe face similar macro-economic problems centering on the impact of deregulation, the collapse of regional trade, severe economic recession and high inflation and the resulting acute social and political unrest. They also share a number of micro-economic problems dealing with industries and markets in which businesses seek to compete and the skills and abilities they have and need to be able to compete effectively (Hooley 1993).

However, many country-specific developments have actually led to uneven progress in the region. Both the industrial heritage of the different Central and Eastern European countries and the individual governments' approach to market reforms–cautious, slow transition, as in the case of Romania, versus complete price liberalization and immediate adoption of a market system in Poland (*CBI News* 1993; Lascu, Manrai and Manrai 1993)–have led to the creation of three levels of development, prompting market analysts to advance the idea of a three-speed Eastern Europe (Lynn 1993). The leaps towards a market system made by countries like Poland, the Czech Republic, Slovenia and Hungary are frequently contrasted with the slower progress achieved by Romania and Bulgaria. Yet a third category is one characterized by economic chaos, which dominates in most of the former Soviet Union, parts of the former Yugoslavia, and Albania.[3]

Three policies have been implemented towards the creation of market economies. One centers on the deregulation of the domestic economy, freeing of international trade and the removal of central planning of quantity and prices and relying on free market forces to enhance productivity (Hooley 1993; Wood and Darling 1993). The second is a policy centering on privatization of state-owned industries and companies on a massive scale (Hooley 1993; Glowacki 1991). The third strategy is a move from outdated, predominantly heavy industrial and agrarian production to more modern and competitive finished goods production, with an emphasis on consumer products (Wood and Darling 1993).

The results of these three strategies have led to very high inflation, as well as high levels of unemployment, rising from a near-zero level during communism, when all citizens of these countries were guaranteed employment, to double-digit levels in countries like Bulgaria, Hungary, Poland, Romania and Slovakia, leading to popular movements questioning the direction in which the reforms are moving, rather than to the creation of post-modern consumers (Firat 1992).

Economic development in Eastern Europe is bound to lead to marketization. In the next section, the concepts of marketization and Westernization will be discussed, along with the placement of the different countries in Central and Eastern Europe on the marketization and Westernization dimensions.

COUNTRY CLUSTERS BASED ON MARKETIZATION AND WESTERNIZATION

Marketization Developments

Marketization has been previously described as the extent to which countries experience dramatic exposure to global communications and dramatic increases in the availability of products, and thereby adapt to these changes by developing institutions promoting privatization.

Some countries have experienced a greater level of marketization than others: Poland, the Czech and Slovak Republics, and Hungary are the countries in the region where consumer desires have been fulfilled to the greatest extent. A reflection of these countries' development level and extent of marketization is also apparent in their expenditure patterns, particularly the percentage of income spent on leisure activities (see Table 3).

These "frontier" countries are followed by countries such as Romania and Bulgaria, where more conservative economic policies, coupled with their forced isolation during Communism, have hindered the transition process. These two countries have recently made great strides to liberalize prices and allow the free circulation of goods; however, the more circum-

TABLE 3. Consumer Expenditure by Product Category (in Percentages)

	Food	Alcoholic Drinks	Non-Alcoholic Drinks	Tobacco	Clothing	Footwear	Housing	Household Fuels	Household Goods & Services	Health	Transport	Leisure	Others	Total
Albania	38.4	5.0	1.8	2.2	7.5	1.4	4.8	4.0	9.8	3.6	6.9	5.2	9.5	100.0
Bulgaria	27.0	11.2	1.0	2.5	7.1	2.5	2.5	2.5	13.6	2.9	8.0	6.6	12.7	100.0
Czech/Slovak Republics	27.2	8.8	1.8	5.2	5.6	1.4	3.6	3.6	14.0	6.6	7.7	4.4	10.1	100.0
Hungary	16.4	6.3	1.3	2.5	3.4	1.5	5.8	2.5	5.5	4.5	6.9	10.9	32.7	100.0
Poland	42.3	1.9		1.6	8.2	2.4	5.1	5.4	3.4	4.3	1.7	11.2	12.3	100.0
Romania	34.1	7.0	2.3	2.3	7.9	2.1	2.6	0.9	2.8	3.2	3.7	6.4	24.7	100.0
Former Yugoslavia	38.9	5.3	1.9	2.5	5.7	3.2	4.4	6.5	4.4	4.1	7.3	4.2	11.7	100.0

Source: *Euromonitor 1993* (for Romania and the Former Yugoslavia). *Euromonitor 1995* (for all other countries).

spect policy they had adopted earlier, as well as the historically limited contact with the West–as will later be seen–still has them lagging behind the "frontier market."

Last in terms of marketization are the republics of the former Soviet Union, the countries of the former Yugoslavia, except Slovenia and Croatia, and Albania–for very different reasons. First, the independent republics of the former Soviet Union, despite their consistent and fervent attempts to adopt a market economy, still have much ground to cover, due to their former economic standing. Albania is considered a lesser developed country by all economic standards, and it is only slowly opening its doors to marketization. Last, the countries of the former Yugoslavia–the federation of the former Eastern bloc which had ranked highest on marketization before the fall of communism in some of its constituent regions–are now, with the exception of Slovenia and Croatia, regressing, rather than advancing economically and from a marketization point of view due to the civil war in the region.

Geopolitical Characteristics and Westernization

Citizens of a country have much in common: they observe the same national holidays and their expenditure will be affected by the economic health of their country; yet, variations in life-styles and priorities are affected by group membership *within* the society at large (Solomon 1996). This is especially true in many countries in Central and Eastern Europe, where borders frequently reflect centuries of expansionary aspirations of Turkey, Russia and, later, the Soviet Union and consequent buffer attempts on the part of the Western world. These push-pull exercises, coupled with, on the most part, failed forced-homogenization efforts, have led to physical boundaries that do not have a homogeneous national content (see Table 2). For example, countries such as Poland and Romania have ethnic majorities in countries that have acquired a quasi-independence from Ukraine and Moldova, respectively.[4] Consequently, the delineation of borders in Central and Eastern Europe partially represents the different nationalities that are contained within the respective borders.

Urbanization also offers a telling picture of the region. An analysis of the level of urbanization may also indicate the extent to which an individual country is likely to succeed in embracing a market economy. Table 2[5] indicates that the Czech and Slovak Republics are the most urbanized of these countries (77.5%), followed by Bulgaria (67.9%), Poland (62%), and Hungary (60.9%). A second category could be constituted by Romania (52.7%) and the countries of the former Yugoslavia (56.1%). The country lagging behind in urbanization in the region is Albania (35.7%), which is also the least developed Central and Eastern European country.

A dimension that should be considered in conjunction with a geo-political analysis is Westernization, that is, the countries' proximity to the West and their history of openness to Western influence. Clearly the countries physically closest to Western Europe, bordering on these highly developed countries, have been less isolated than the countries located in the far Eastern region of the continent. Those countries that have allowed the greatest level of influence to penetrate and affect the population during the days of communism, through media and tourism (Goszczynska, Tyszka and Slovic 1991), for instance, have acquired many of the values and aspirations of Western consumers. These countries were Czechoslovakia, Hungary, Poland and Yugoslavia. (Yugoslavia had actually gained a reputation in the region–positive for individuals who welcomed Western influence and negative for its censors–for maintaining an open border with Italy in the town of Trieste.) Consequently, these same newly-marketizing countries are characterized by a higher level of Westernization, compared to their neighbors to the East, as well as Albania.

Rating lower on Westernization are Romania and Bulgaria, which, although not as isolated as the former Soviet Union, have experienced a more controlled environment, where contact with foreign influences, in person, through media, etc., was greatly restricted. Yet in a third category in terms of isolation were the Soviet Union and Albania, which strictly monitored and severely limited access to Western influence.

The extent of Westernization is still obvious in the trading partners that each of the countries in the region have selected. The least Westernized countries still have the greatest amount of trade with the former countries of the Council of Mutual Economic Assistance (CMEA), comprised of other Central and Eastern European communist countries (Table 2). However, this situation is in a continuous change; for example, the Baltic States are at an advantage, compared to the other former Soviet Republics. They are receiving extensive support from developed Scandinavian countries in their transition efforts.

THE MARKETIZATION-WESTERNIZATION POSITIONING MATRIX: IMPLICATIONS FOR MARKETING PRACTITIONERS

Mapping the countries of the former Eastern Europe in terms of the degree (from low to high) to which they had historically experienced Western influence and in terms of the extent (from low to high) to which they are successful in their marketizing efforts, we obtain the four clusters (see Figures 1 and 2).

The first cluster, containing highly-marketized, highly-Westernized countries (the Czech and Slovak Republics, Hungary, Poland and Slovenia), appears to be most attractive to foreign investors. It seems that this cluster has fewer impediments to foreign direct investment and ownership than any other cluster. This market is not only attractive for its high degree of development and consequent consumer earning power; as a more urbanized region, it offers easier access to the market via its large capital cities and regional metropolis. Moreover, the region boasts a rising entrepreneurial class that has recently posed serious competitive threats to Western market entrants by providing similar products and services at much lower prices than their Western counterparts.

Certain unifying characteristics of this market, such as religion and the region's Slavic consistuency, allow for a relatively uniform accessibility of the market. For instance, marketers may use regiocentric appeals that only need minimal modifications in translation to appeal to the entire market.

The second cluster, lower-marketizing, highly-Westernized countries (Bosnia-Herzegovina, Montenegro, Macedonia, Serbia and Croatia), will offer great potential to marketers once it stabilizes. While certain differences will continue to exist–religion, for instance, may require marketers to meet market needs differently–this market will probably lend itself to similar approaches to those used in the first cluster, if it overcomes its current conflicts.

The higher-marketizing, less-Westernized countries (Bulgaria and Romania) continue to be approached with caution by Western entrants. While the major players in most product and service categories have already engaged in extensive direct investment, lesser international players are still adopting a wait-and-see attitude. Moreover, these countries are grappling with corruption and internal conflicts–ethnic and political–rendering them a more risky endeavor for investors.

Finally, the lower marketizing, less-Westernized cluster (the Western countries of the Former Soviet Union and Albania[6]) presents the highest risk to investors. Despite the uniform accessibility of the countries of the Former Soviet Union–one common language (Russian), cultural similarity, equal development–these countries have not yet been heavily courted by Western businesses. Nevertheless, they too present a high potential as a market with a high literacy rate, cheap labor, and an insatiable desire for Western goods. It is, in fact, worth mentioning that this category is characterized by greater within-cluster variance divergence. For example, Russia, although not Westernized, has made significant progress in its marketization, ahead of the other countries of the Commonwealth of Independent States. At the same time, the Baltic countries (themselves not

FIGURE 1. Marketization-Westernization Country Clusters

Cluster 1: *Highly-Marketized, Highly-Westernized Countries*:
The Czech and Slovak Republics, Hungary, Poland, Slovenia
Characteristics:
Geographic	-located in Central Europe, and border developed countries
	-more urbanized
Cultural	-Slavic languages, with one exception (Hungary)
	-primarily Catholic religion
Economic	-more developed

Cluster 2: *Lower-Marketized, Highly-Westernized Countries*:
The countries of the former Yugoslavia: Bosnia-Herzegovina, Monternegro, Macedonia, Serbia, Croatia
Characteristics:
Geographic	-located in the Central Europe
	-more urbanized
Cultural	-Slavic languages
	-primarily Eastern Orthodox religion; Muslim
Economic	-more developed, but at war, under boycott

Cluster 3: *Higher-Marketized, Less-Westernized Countries*:
Bulgaria and Romania
Characteristics:
Geographic	-located in the Balkan Peninsula, at the "gates of the Orient"
	-urbanized to a lesser extent than Cluster 2
Cultural	-Latin and Slavic languages
	-Eastern Orthodox religion
Economic	-slower in the development process

Cluster 4: *Lower-Marketized, Less- Westernized Countries*:
Albania, the Western countries of the Former Soviet Union
Characteristics:
Geographic	-urbanized to a lesser extent than Cluster 3
Cultural	-Slavic languages—Russia is the primary commercial language
	-Eastern Orthodox and Muslim religions
Economic	-formerly "fierce" dictatorships
	-slower development

a homogeneous group) have strong historical and cultural ties to the West. Further, Estonia, one of the fastest-growing economies in the region, is undertaking great efforts at marketization and will soon be a candidate for the high-marketizing cluster.

CONCLUSION

The clusters of countries described above are likely to have certain characteristics that cut across the former national boundaries, and share similar consumer needs and purchasing behavior. We propose four main

FIGURE 2. Marketization and Westernization in Central and Eastern Europe

Cluster 1: The Czech and Slovak Republics, Hungary, Poland, Slovenia

Cluster 2: Countries of the Former Yugoslavia (Mecedonia, Montenegro, Serbia, Croatia, Bosnia-Herzegovina)

Cluster 3: Bulgaria and Romania

Cluster 4: Albania, the Independent Republics of the Former Soviet Union

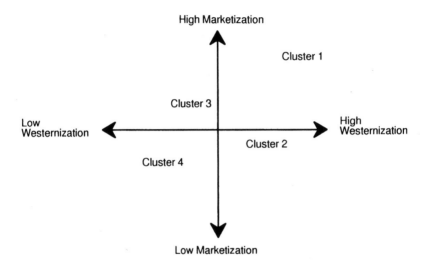

Central and Eastern European country clusters, based on the marketization and Westernization dimensions. These clusters also share a number of characteristics that can be described in terms of economic development and culture–the dimensions traditionally used in describing these emerging markets.

A dimension that may further be considered by future research is the starting point of the marketization-Westernization dimensions. That is, the temporal dimension merits inclusion in the analysis: it would be interesting to note, over time, what countries have made more progress than others relative to the initial starting point. In this sense, it is also worth noting that it is easier for countries to progress on the marketization dimension, while the degree of Westernization is more difficult to change, since such change entails change in the culture itself.

Finally, while micro, brand-specific decisions will not be fully addressed by the proposed dimensions given the country-level specializations for certain products (glass industry in the Czech Republic and food production in Hungary, for example), it is herein argued that the segmentation dimensions suggested above are superior to geographic, demographic or psychographic segmentation criteria for the Central and Eastern European market. First, they are directly relevant to the marketizing process in the economies in the region. Secondly, they capture simultaneously the dimensions of economic development, culture, history and the degree of market orientation. As such, the marketization-Westernization matrix is herein advanced as a starting point for marketing managers in their effort to segment the Central and Eastern European market.

NOTES

1. Since the profile of Central and Eastern Europe is constantly changing, and the republics of the former Soviet Union and the former Yugoslavia do not all yet have a clearly defined status, this study will address the newly-independent republics in conjunction with the various developments in the larger respective former federation. The readers must also be cautioned that the disruptions in these particular sub-regions have represented a substantial impediment to the collection of recent and reliable information by research providers.

2. The present article excludes the newly-independent Asian republics of the Commonwealth of Independent States, where the Muslim religion is predominant.

3. It should be noted, however, that Albania has recently made noteworthy economic leaps.

4. Moldova, for instance, has a Romanian majority (65%), while the language imposed on the population continues to be Russian.

5. Table 2 illustrates a number of relevant data on the countries to be explored in this study. No information is yet available for the Czech Republic and for Slovakia individually; thus, they are still treated as a unit–Czechoslovakia.

6. Albania's current effort for rapid marketization renders it a likely candidate for Cluster 3.

REFERENCES

Belk, Russel W. and Guliz Ger (1994). Problems of Marketization in Romania and Turkey. In C. Schultz, R. Belk, and G. Ger (Eds.), *Research in Consumer Behavior*, Vol. 7, pp. 123-156.

CBI News (1993). Initiative Eastern Europe: Special Report on Poland, The Confederation of British Industry, June.

Department of State Dispatch (1995). U.S. Department of State, Country Profiles.

European Marketing Data and Statistics. Euromonitor Plc., London, Great Britain, 1993.

European Marketing Data and Statistics. Euromonitor Plc., London, Great Britain, 1995.

Firat, Fuat A. (1992). Post-Modernism and the Marketing Organization, *Journal of Organizational Change Management*, Vol. 5, No. 1, 79-83.

Ger, Guliz, Russell Belk and Dana-Nicoleta Lascu (1993). The Development of Consumer Desire in Marketizing and Developing Economies: The Cases of Romania and Turkey. In *Advances in Consumer Research*, Leigh McAlister and Michael Rothchild (Eds.), Vol. 20, Provo, Utah: Association for Consumer Research, pp. 102-107.

Glowacki, R. (1991). State of the Market Structure and Its Implications, *International Studies of Management and Organizations*, Vol. 21, 39-58.

Goszczynska, Maryla, Tadeusz Tyszka and Paul Slovic (1991). Risk Perception in Poland: A Comparison with Three Other Countries, *Journal of Behavioral Decision Making*, Vol. 4, 179-193.

Hooley, Graham J. (1993). Raising the Iron Curtain: Marketing in a Period of Transition, *European Journal of Marketing*, Vol. 27, 11/12, 6-20.

Keyfitz, Nathan and Robert A. Dorfman (1991). *The Market Economy is the Best But Not the Easiest* (mimeograph), 7-13.

Lascu, Dana-Nicoleta, Lalita A. Manrai and Ajay K. Manrai (1994a). Status-Concern and Consumer Purchase Behavior in the Marketizing Economy of Romania: From the Legacies of Prescribed Consumption to the Fantasies of Desired Acquisition. In C. Shultz, R. Belk, and G. Ger (Eds.) *Research in Consumer Behavior*, Vol. 7, pp. 89-122.

Lascu, Dana-Nicoleta, Lalita A. Manrai and Ajay K. Manrai (1994b). Emerging Issues for Marketing in Central and Eastern Europe: An Analysis of Marketization-Westernization Country Clusters. Paper presented at the 19th Annual Macromarketing Conference, Boulder, Colorado.

Lascu, Dana-Nicoleta, Lalita A. Manrai and Ajay K. Manrai (1993). Marketing in Romania: The Challenges of the Transition from a Centrally-Planned Economy to a Consumer-Oriented Economy, *European Journal of Marketing*, Vol. 27, 11/12, 102-120.

Lynn, Jonathan (1993). *The Reuter European Business Report*, BC Cycle, August 3.

Manrai, Lalita A., Ajay J. Manrai and Dana-Nicoleta Lascu. Eastern Europe's Transition to Market Economy, An Analysis of Economic and Political Risks, *Journal of Euromarketing*, Vol. 4.

Solomon, Michael R. (1996). *Consumer Behavior*, Second Edition, Englewood Cliffs, NJ: Prentice Hall.

Vandermerwe, Sandra and Marc-Andre L'Huiller (1990). Euro-Consumers in 1992, In *Marketing Strategies for the New Europe: A North American Perspective on 1992*, John K. Ryans Jr. and Pradeep A. Rau, Chicago, IL: American Marketing Association, 151-164.

Wood, Van R. and John R. Darling (1993). The Marketing Challenge of the Newly Independent Republics: Product Competitiveness in Global Markets, *Journal of International Marketing*, Vol. 1, 1.

Market-Entry Strategies in Poland– A Preliminary Report

Shaukat Ali
Hafiz Mirza

SUMMARY. This paper reports findings of a study undertaken on market-entry strategies of UK firms in Poland. It presents a cross sectional profile of UK firms investing in Poland, their motives for entering the Polish market, and their entry strategies and assesses their performance in terms of their entry strategies and experiences with regard to financial, technological, marketing and strategic aspects. The paper compares the findings with international market-entry theory and concludes by examining managerial implications of the study. *[Article copies available for a fee from The Haworth Document Delivery Service: 1-800-342-9678. E-mail address: getinfo@haworth.com]*

INTRODUCTION

Following the collapse of communism in the late 1980s, Central and Eastern Europe opened up previously undreamed-of opportunities for Western firms. Virtually overnight, a vast market of huge potential suddenly

---

Shaukat Ali is affiliated with the University of Bradford, the Management Center, Bradford, West Yorkshire, UK.

Hafiz Mirza is Professor in the Management Centre, University of Bradford, Bradford, West Yorkshire, UK.

An earlier version of this paper was presented at the Third Annual Conference on Marketing Strategies for Central and Eastern Europe in Vienna, November/ December 1995.

[Haworth co-indexing entry note]: "Market-Entry Strategies in Poland–A Preliminary Report." Ali, Shaukat, and Hafiz Mirza. Co-published simultaneously in *Journal of East-West Business* (International Business Press, an imprint of The Haworth Press, Inc.) Vol. 3, No. 1, 1996, pp. 43-62; and: *Marketing in Central and Eastern Europe* (ed: Jan Nowak) International Business Press, an imprint of The Haworth Press, Inc., 1996, pp. 43-62. Single or multiple copies of this article are available for a fee from The Haworth Document Delivery Service [1-800-342-9678, 9:00 a.m. - 5:00 p.m. (EST). E-mail address: getinfo@haworth.com].

43

opened up. Western Europe had on its doorstep a market larger than either the European Union or the USA, and one with a vast untapped potential.

It was generally believed that central to the strategy for releasing the vast potential of the region–to the benefit of the West and the East European countries–was co-operation. At the political level, this took the form of the Association Agreement signed, or under negotiation, between a number of the nations of Central and Eastern Europe and the European Union. These agreements will in time lead to the progressive trade liberalization across the whole of the new Europe, and in due course to a single market bordering Russia (Pinder, 1993; Tovias, 1994).

In addition, multinational institutions and their constituent governments have been actively providing know-how, expertise and finance to overcome difficulties associated with the inadequate framework–legal, fiscal and institutional–for business development in Central and Eastern Europe. Ample examples exist to support this, evidenced by the growing number of joint ventures with businesses from the West; in Western banks, investing directly in companies in Central Europe; and, in legal and accountancy firms, providing advice on such issues as privatization, etc., to the governments of the region. Also, it is widely accepted that the development of a healthy small and medium enterprise sector is essential for the creation of a market economy in the countries of Central and Eastern Europe. A vital role in this process is played by external investment, which brings with it much-needed management skills and technical know-how.

Since the transition to a free market economy, substantial foreign direct investment (FDI) has occurred in Central and Eastern Europe, both demand and supply led (Artisien et al., 1993; Buckley and Ghauri, 1994; Engholm, 1993; Howell, 1994; Johnson and Loveman, 1995; Paliwoda, 1995; Shama, 1995; Williams, 1993). Governments and local firms have been eager to benefit from transfers in capital, technology and managerial skills. Foreign firms, led by multinationals, have been eager to pursue new growth opportunities (Egan et al., 1995; Shama, 1995).

Companies seeking to expand into foreign markets have a choice of entry modes, ranging from exporting, licensing, franchising, management contracts, joint ventures, strategic alliances, and wholly-owned subsidiaries among others. These strategies are distinguished by the degree of investment and the risk-investment potential (Cateora, 1993; Paliwoda, 1993; Young et al., 1989). Existing studies on the internationalization process of firms suggest that firms proceed in a consistent stepwise fashion along some continuum as they develop their international activities (Kim and Hwang, 1992; Root, 1987; Turnbull, 1987; Strandskov, 1986; Welch and Luostarinen, 1988; Young et al., 1989). This incremental movement through various stages of learning, commitment, has undergone substantial study (Buckley and Casson, 1981; Cavusgil, 1980; Johanson and Wiedersheim-Paul, 1975; Kaynak, 1988; Falbe and Dandrdige, 1992; Root, 1987; Tookey, 1969; Wind, Douglas and Perlmutter, 1973). Most of the empirical data involved in the above studies was derived from firms going into developed markets, over relatively long periods of time.

To what extent do these theories explain investment in Central and Eastern Europe, where markets opened up almost overnight, providing unpredicted and uncertain opportunities, which furthermore, due to competitive pressures, required rapid market entry through FDI (Healey, 1994)? A substantial body of literature addresses the motives for FDI (Beamish and Banks, 1987; Brewer 1993; Buckley, 1989; Buckley and Casson, 1976; Casson, 1987; Dunning and Rugman, 1985; Dunning, 1988; Harrigan 1986; Hennart, 1988, 1991a, 1991b; Lecraw, 1992; Paliwoda, 1993; Rugman and Verbeke, 1991; Terpstra and Yu, 1988), ranging from pre-empting competitors, following competitors, following clients, geographical diversity, achieving economies of scale, exploiting host government provisions, to utilizing outdated technology, etc.

Given the above, while knowledge of the appropriate transnational entry strategies (by both large and SMEs) into industrialized markets and many parts of the developing world is well established, this is not the case in Central and Eastern Europe. Indeed, because significant foreign investment into this region is occurring for the first time in the post war era, much can be learned about the "primary" mechanisms, motives, etc., of multinational firms. Hence while previous studies on the internationalization process were developed and tested on familiar markets, Central and Eastern Europe, with its unique characteristics, offers unique opportunities to explore changing patterns of investment.

British firms, although slow in getting started, have responded to the challenge and invested significantly in Central and Eastern Europe. This paper presents the results from a cross-section of British firms which have invested in Poland. In particular, the paper focuses on the motives for investing in Poland, the nature of the entry strategies, and performance with regard to financial and marketing aspects.

METHOD

The research instrument was a mail questionnaire, developed after an extensive literature review. It was reviewed by four academics and piloted during the autumn of 1994. The questionnaire was divided into 7 parts (background information, investment motivation and strategy, modes of entry, ownership and financing, organization management and control, performance evaluation and general policy issues). The pilot study resulted in a revised questionnaire, containing 54 open-and-closed ended questions, which was mailed to individuals, either in the UK or Poland, who had agreed previously to participate in the survey. The companies involved were of different sizes, ranging from small to major multinationals, spread across many industry sectors. The original database contained over 250 British firms with investments in Poland. Preliminary work identified shelf companies, investment by UK-based, though non-UK registered, multinationals, firms having relocated, closed down, etc., were subsequently removed from the list, leaving a sample of 225 companies.

In a limited number of cases, both home and host country addresses of the firms involved were available, some with contact names, mainly local staff; however, the vast majority had no contact names. To save costs on mailing, printing of questionnaires, avoiding reminders, as well as improving the response rate, a letter was sent, enclosing a pre-addressed fax form, to each company in the host country, explaining the purpose of the research and asking for a contact name, either in the UK or in Poland if appropriate, who could assist.

Following the faxed responses, 52 firms refused to co-operate for reasons of confidentiality, lack of time or staff or inappropriateness of their firm to the study. A further 17 letters were returned unopened, indicating the firms had closed down, relocated, etc. Questionnaires were subsequently sent to the remaining 156 firms. A reminder was then sent, followed by a second wave of questionnaires. A final reminder was sent three months later. In total 35 usable questionnaires were returned, representing a response rate of 22.4%, which is acceptable given the length and complexity of the questionnaire (Hart, 1987).

FINDINGS

The research sought to ascertain the nature and experiences of UK firms in Poland, focusing on senior managers. Table 1 shows the functional positions of the respondents. The vast majority of the respondents were marketing managers/directors (28.6%), although a significant proportion (14.3%) were Chief Executive Officers (CEOs), with a similar number being sales managers/directors. It is interesting that a relatively large number of CEOs chose to answer the questionnaire personally, indicating that not only are strategic investment decisions being made at the top, as one would expect, but also, surprisingly, that management at the highest levels is personally monitoring the investment outcome and has direct knowledge of the business. Another significant finding is that a comparatively large number of respondents are partners in the UK firms; some of these

TABLE 1. Functional position of respondent.

Position of respondents	Number of Respondents	Percent
Chief Executive Officer	5	14.3
Marketing Manager/Director	10	28.6
Sales Manager/Director	5	14.3
Financial Director	3	8.6
Director/GM-Central Europe	4	11.4
Commercial Manager	1	2.9
Partner	4	11.4
Regional Manager	1	2.9
Manager Business Planning	1	2.9
Central Europe Finance Manager	1	2.9
TOTAL	**35**	**100.0**

partners were in consulting firms/auditing firms, others small owner managed businesses.

Companies responding to the survey included a number of banks, publishers, manufacturing and construction firms, business and management consultants, insurance and financial services; in all, more than 20 separate business categories are represented as shown in Table 2.

The business category most represented is banking and licensed deposit takers (8.6%). Most of the major clearing banks in the UK refused to participate in the survey, citing confidentiality as the main reason. The banks represented in the survey are investment banks. This reluctance on the part UK banks to divulge information is in sharp contrast to German banks (Ali, 1996a), the vast majority of which were quite willing to answer most questions.

Developing the profile of respondents further, Table 3a gives an indication of the size of the UK firms participating in the survey, in terms of the number of employees. The largest single categories of firms (22.9%) were those with employees greater than 30,000. Clearly these were major multinational companies, with considerable international business experience. The significance of this experience will become apparent later, when the market entry strategies are examined. The next largest category (8.6%) consists of firms with employees between 10,000-19,000; however, the vast majority of the firms in the survey (more than 62%) had fewer than 10,000 employees, of which 5.7% had fewer than 10.

TABLE 2. Business activities of participating firms.

Business category	Number of Respondents	Percent
Banks and licensed deposit takers	3	8.6
Printing and publishing	2	5.7
Chemical and Allied products	2	5.7
Rubber and Plastics	2	5.7
Pharmaceuticals (Manufacturing)	2	5.7
Business/management services	2	5.7
Engineering consultants	2	5.7
Construction contractors	1	2.9
Water proofing products (Construction)	1	2.9
Insurance Carriers	1	2.9
Insurance Brokers	1	2.9
Petroleum Refining	1	2.9
Primary metals	1	2.9
Industrial and Commercial machinery	1	2.9
Metal Processing	1	2.9
Wholesale-durable goods	1	2.9
Import/Export	1	2.9
Passenger Transportation	1	2.9
Telecommunications	1	2.9
Telecommunications Consulting	1	2.9
Hotels/Catering	1	2.9
Legal Services	1	2.9
Accounting/Auditing	1	2.9
Architecture	1	2.9
Research/IT in Maritime environment	1	2.9
Surveying	1	2.9
Construction consulting	1	2.9
TOTAL	**35.0**	**100.0**

TABLE 3a. Number of employees of U.K. parent firms.

Number of employees- (parent firm)	Number of Respondents	Percent	Cum Percent
0-9	2	5.7	6.1
10-19	1	2.9	8.6
20-29	1	2.9	11.4
40-49	1	2.9	14.3
50-74	1	2.9	17.1
75-99	2	5.7	22.9
150-199	1	2.9	25.7
200-299	1	2.9	28.6
300-399	2	5.7	34.3
400-499	1	2.9	37.1
600-799	1	2.9	40.0
800-999	1	2.9	42.9
2,000-2,499	1	2.9	45.7
3,500-3,999	2	5.7	51.4
4,000-4,999	2	5.7	57.1
5,000-9,999	2	5.7	62.9
10,000-19,000	3	8.6	71.4
20,000-29,000	2	5.7	77.1
>30,000	8	22.9	100.0
TOTAL	**35**	**100.0**	

Table 3b shows the corresponding size of the affiliates in Poland. As the table shows, the vast majority of affiliates (more than 74%) have fewer than 50 employees, with 2 firms (5.7%) having between 600-799 employees. Only one firm had what might be termed large operations (in excess of 3,000 employees), resulting from an acquisition.

Table 4a indicates the size of the UK firms signified by their annual revenues. Again major multinationals are presented by 22.9% of them having total revenues greater than US$3 billion. At the other extreme, 8.6% of the respondents had annual revenues of less than US$3 million. The corresponding results for the affiliates are shown in Table 4b. The significance of Table 4b is that more than 62% of the affiliates in Poland had annual revenues of less than US$3 million, indicating that the affiliates are still comparatively small.

TABLE 3b. Number of employees of Polish affiliates.

Number of employees- (Polish affiliate)	Number of Respondents	Percent	Cum Percent
0-9	13	37.1	37.1
10-19	8	22.9	60.1
20-29	2	5.7	65.7
30-39	2	5.7	71.4
40-49	1	2.9	74.3
50-74	1	2.9	77.1
75-99	1	2.9	80.0
150-199	1	2.9	82.9
200-299	1	2.9	85.7
400-499	1	2.9	88.6
500-599	1	2.9	91.4
600-799	2	5.7	97.1
3,000-3,499	1	2.9	100.0
TOTAL	**35**	**100.0**	

Table 5 shows the various years in which market entry took place. One firm indicated that they had been doing business in Poland for over 30 years. However the vast majority of the sample firms (57.1%) entered the Polish market during 1991-92, some two years after the fall of Communism in the region. This shows that many UK firms were perhaps too cautious in entering the market, to their competitive disadvantage, in comparison with their German competitors (Ali, 1995a).

Table 6 illustrates how the firms investing in Poland have also invested in other countries in Eastern and Central Europe. Whilst 40% of the firms had investments in Poland only, the remaining 60% also had investments in other countries in the region, as well as Poland. A significant 20% of the firms had investments in all three "advanced" countries of Poland, Czech Republic and Hungary, with another 20% having investments in these three countries and Russia. Over 77% of those sampled had investments in the three Central European countries.

The questionnaire asked respondents the reasons for investing in Poland; respondents were presented with a range of factors identified from the literature. They were also given the opportunity to state other reasons not listed. The results are shown in Table 7. There was a combination of reasons, most important of those chosen from the list given was Poland

TABLE 4a. Annual revenues of U.K. firms.

Annual revenue of parent firm (US$m)*	Number of Respondents	Percent	Cum Percent
0-2.9	3	8.6	8.6
3-5.9	3	8.6	17.2
15-29	3	8.6	25.8
30-44	2	5.7	31.4
60-74	1	2.9	34.3
75-111	1	2.9	37.1
112-149	2	5.7	42.9
150-299	2	5.7	48.6
300-374	1	2.9	51.4
600-674	2	5.7	57.1
675-749	1	2.9	60.0
1,200-1,499	2	5.7	65.7
1,500-2,249	2	5.7	71.4
2,250-2,999	2	5.7	77.1
>3,000	8	22.9	100.0
TOTAL	**35**	**100.0**	

*Converted from £ sterling at the rate of £1 = US$1.5

being a 'strategic location,' cited to be between 'quite important' and 'very important.' Further significant reasons cited were to obtain higher profits, market penetration, to pre-empt competitors and establish a local image. However, none of the reasons cited in the literature were thought to be 'extremely important,' constituting the primary motive for investing in Poland. The four reasons cited as being 'extremely important' were: good local entrepreneur, to follow clients, availability of complimentary technical expertise, and market size/potential. However these reasons were cited by only one respondent in each case.

Table 8 shows the entry methods used by the firms when investing in Poland. The figures indicate the dynamics of various strategies as the firms develop their operations. As a first step strategy, 30.3% of the firms used exporting, with agency and wholly-owned subsidiary both being used by 24.2% of the firms. Majority joint ventures were also used as a first step entry by 20.6% of firms, while significantly minority joint venture was only used in one case. The implication here is that for an equity stake, firms prefer to have ownership control. This is further shown by the

TABLE 4b. Annual revenues of the Polish affiliates.

Annual revenue of host venture (US$m)*	Number of Respondents	Percent	Cum Percent
0-2.9	22	62.9	62.9
3-4.4	3	8.6	71.4
4.5-5.9	1	2.9	74.3
6-7.4	2	5.7	80.0
7.5-14.9	1	2.9	82.9
15-21	2	5.7	88.6
22-29	1	2.9	91.4
30-44	1	2.9	94.3
45-59	1	2.9	97.1
112-149	1	2.9	100.0
TOTAL	**35**	**100.0**	

*Converted from £ sterling at the rate of £1 = US$1.5

TABLE 5. Year of investment in Poland.

Year of investment in Poland	Number of Respondents	Percent	Cum Percent
Pre-1970	1	2.9	2.9
1976-80	2	5.7	8.9
1981-85	1	2.9	11.4
1986-90	7	20.0	31.4
1991-92	20	57.1	88.6
1993-94	4	11.4	100.0
TOTAL	**35**	**100.0**	

fact that in steps two and three, the number of wholly owned subsidiaries has increased at each step so that, by the third step, more than 60% of the firms had wholly owned subsidiaries.

Comparing the dynamics of these market entry strategies with the internationalization process proposed by the Uppsala School (Johanson and Weidersheim-Paul, 1975; Johanson and Vahlne, 1997; Vahlne and Nordstrom, 1988), it is clear that there are significant differences between their *establishment chain* and the behavior of firms in Poland. The Uppsala Model argues internationalization is the increasing degree of involvement

TABLE 6. Countries of investment.

Country of Investment	No. of Respondents	Percent	Cum Percent
Poland	14	40.0	40.0
Hungary and Poland	2	5.7	45.7
Hungary, Poland and the Czech Republic	7	20.0	65.7
Poland and Slovakia	1	2.9	68.6
All of the above and Slovakia	3	8.6	77.1
All of the above and Russia	7	20.0	97.1
Poland, the Czech Republic and Slovakia	1	2.9	100
TOTAL	**35**	**100.0**	

by firms in foreign markets, with implications for both the size of resource commitment and the acquisition of market information. In the case of Poland, over 40% of the firms used majority equity modes as an initial entry method, while those employing exporting and agency representation quickly changed their modes within a year or so in light of their experience. Furthermore, there is little evidence to support the concept of "psychic distance" as proposed by Dunning (1981 p. 102). The findings show that, given the dynamics of international business in the region, it is market opportunities that dictate entry modes, and not necessarily psychic considerations.

Another interesting point in Table 8 is that both licensing and turnkey entry were not used at all. The reasons for not using licensing can only be speculated on. Licensing requires a partner capable of using the technology, which may not be evident; also the dynamics of the region to a large extent dictate equity investment. The use of turnkey operations is very much dependent on large scale infrastructure projects, which, for the present, do not appear to be planned. Similarly, franchising has not been used to any significant extent, in spite of 'good local entrepreneurs,' possibly due to a lack of suitable franchisees.

The respondents were asked to assess the performance of their Polish affiliates in terms of financial and marketing aspects in comparison with their expectations at the start of the venture. The results are shown in Table 9.

The findings show a mixed combination, with different perceptions for different factors. With regard to the financial measures, over 64% of the

TABLE 7. Reasons for investing in Poland.

Factors	Rank	Mean Score	S.D.
A strategic location	1	3.60	1.22
To obtain additional profits or higher margins	2	3.55	1.43
Market penetration	3	3.23	1.61
Pre-empt competitors	4	3.03	1.57
Establish local image	4	3.03	1.48
Reduce financial risk	5	2.82	1.61
Existence of a more developed market/business environment	6	2.67	1.34
Availability of skilled labour	7	2.62	1.56
Geographical diversification	8	2.49	1.40
Better infrastructure	9	2.44	1.35
Third party invitation	10	2.35	1.65
Lower labour costs	10	2.35	1.45
Psychic/cultural proximity	11	2.06	1.52
Exploit government investment provisions	12	1.97	1.43
Follow competitors	13	1.94	1.30
Gain access to distribution network	14	1.91	1.48
Availability of better local support industries	15	1.85	1.46
Assure raw material supply	16	1.68	1.34
Protect and sell patents/licenses	17	1.62	2.37
Overcome import barriers	18	1.59	1.23
Overcome tariffs	18	1.59	1.26
Utilize outdated technology	19	1.56	1.38
Reduce transport costs	20	1.50	1.24
Additional factors stated by respondents	Rank	Mean Score	S.D
Market size/potential	1	5.00	0.00
Good local entrepreneur	1	5.00	0.00
To follow clients	1	5.00	0.00
Availability of complimentary technical expertise	1	5.00	0.00
Local knowledge (knew country well)	2	3.00	0.00
Existing Polish contacts in London	2	3.00	0.00

importance of each factor: 1 = not at all important, 2 = not very important, 3 = quite important, 4 = very important, 5 = extremely important

TABLE 8. Type of market entry used to enter Poland.

Method of entry*	1st step	2nd step	3rd step	Not used	No response
Exporting	10 (30.3%)	1 (3.0%)	1 (3.0%)	21 (63.6%)	2
Agency	8 (24.2%)	2 (6.1%)	–	23 (69.7%)	2
Wholly-owned subsidiary	8 (24.2%)	6 (18.2%)	7 (21.2%)	12 (36.4%)	2
Majority joint venture	6 (17.6%)	7 (20.6%)	2 (5.9%)	19 (55.9%)	1
Minority joint venture	1 (2.9%)	1 (2.9%)	2 (5.7%)	29 (82.9%)	2
Licensing	-	-	-	33 (100%)	2
Turnkey operation	–	–	–	33 (100%)	2
Management contract	2 (5.7%)	–	–	31 (93.9%)	2
Technical co-operation	1 (3.0%)	3 (9.1%)	–	29 (87.9%)	2
Franchising	1 (2.9%)	-	-	32 (97.0%)	2
Import from Poland**	1 (2.9%)	–	–	N/A	–
Representative office**	–	2 (2.9%)	–	N/A	–

* multiple entries were undertaken in some cases
* * added by the respondents and not on the questionnaire

respondents indicated that their sales levels were favorable (21.2% 'as expected,' 21.2% 'better than expected' and 24.2% 'much better than expected'). However, a significant 18.2% thought their sales levels were either worse than expected or much worse than expected. For profitability, a larger number, 27.3%, had unfavorable results. Just over 54% of the respondents perceived their performance as expected or better. Figures for cost control and pay-back period show a similar picture. The noteworthy aspect about the financial indicators is the relatively high percentage of firms which indicated 'not applicable' for the various categories (just over 15%). Clearly firms are using other measures for success and these require further analysis. Furthermore, it has to be remembered these figures are not absolute but relative to expectations prior to investment. Hence, the successful performance of the businesses with regard to financial aspects can be explained in one of two ways. Either the businesses are genuinely performing well, or firms had been, perhaps, too pessimistic in the beginning and set lower targets for themselves.

TABLE 9. Performance of the Polish operations.

Factors	No. of Respondents	Percent	Mean Score	S.D.
FINANCIAL ASPECTS				
Sales level			3.88	1.52
Much worse than expected	3	9.1		
Worse than expected	3	9.1		
As expected	7	21.2		
Better than expected	7	21.2		
Much better than expected	8	24.2		
Not applicable	5	15.2		
	2	Missing		
Profitability			3.61	1.60
Much worse than expected	2	6.1		
Worse than expected	7	21.2		
As expected	9	27.3		
Better than expected	6	18.2		
Much better than expected	3	9.1		
Not applicable	5	15.2		
Confidential	1	3.0		
	2	Missing		
Cost control			3.5	1.5
Much worse than expected	1	3.1		
Worse than expected	6	17.18		
As expected	15	46.9		
Better than expected	3	9.4		
Much better than expected	1	3.1		
Not applicable	5	15.6		
Confidential	1	3.1		
	3	Missing		
Pay-back period			3.58	1.74
Much worse than expected	2	7.7		
Worse than expected	5	19.2		
As expected	10	38.5		
Better than expected	1	3.8		
Much better than expected	2	7.7		
Not applicable	5	19.2		
Confidential	1	3.8		
	9	Missing		

TABLE 9 (continued)

Factors	No. of Respondents	Percent	Mean Score	S.D.
MARKETING ASPECTS				
Market share			3.91	1.38
Much worse than expected	2	6.1		
Worse than expected	3	9.1		
As expected	5	15.2		
Better than expected	15	45.5		
Much better than expected	2	6.1		
Not applicable	6	18.2		
	2	Missing		
Advertisement/promotion			4.00	1.34
Much worse than expected	1	3.4		
As expected	12	41.4		
Better than expected	8	27.6		
Much better than expected	1	3.4		
Not applicable	7	24.1		
	6	Missing		
Distribution			4.10	1.45
Much worse than expected	1	3.4		
Worse than expected	1	3.4		
As expected	10	34.5		
Better than expected	8	27.6		
Not applicable	9	31.0		
	6	Missing		
Reputation			4.133	1.11
As expected	10	33.3		
Better than expected	12	40.0		
Much better than expected	2	6.7		
Not applicable	6	20.0		
	5	Missing		
Customer service			4.17	1.2
As expected	12	40.0		
Better than expected	8	26.7		
Much better than expected	3	10.0		
Not applicable	7	23.3		
	5	Missing		

1 = much worse than expected, 2 = worse than expected, 3 = as expected, 4 = better than expected, 5 = much better than expected

With respect to marketing aspects, for all five categories represented (market share, advertisement/promotion, distribution, reputation and customer service), the respondent's perceptions were favorable in comparison to earlier expectations. Given the diversity of the firms represented in the sample, not all categories were relevant, hence the relatively high number of 'not applicable' responses. Over 60% of the respondents had favorable market share, while firms' expectations for advertising and promotion seemed realistic, with just over 41% of the respondents indicating effectiveness 'as expected.' Similar figures for distribution, reputation, and customer service confirm the previous statement that UK firms were perhaps unnecessarily pessimistic in their expectations in entering the Polish market, and were surprised at the success of the ventures.

Respondents were asked to rate the overall performance of their investment. Their responses are shown in Table 10. Just over 47% of the investments appear to have met the firms' expectations, with a further 17.6 % and 11.8% having exceeded their expectations and highly exceeded their expectations respectively. This, of course, does not necessarily equate with profitability or other measures thought to signify success. Different firms have different expectations; for some it was to establish a local presence before setting up a wholly-owned subsidiary. So while the venture lost money, it met expectations. Whilst a significant number stated that the venture had failed their expectations (14.7%), qualitative insights from the respondents indicate that these were due to conflicts between joint venture partners (Ali, 1996b). A small number of investments (8.6%) were in their early stages, hence proper evaluation could not be made.

Encouragingly, their future plans are positive as Table 11 shows. When asked what their future plans were in the near future, slightly fewer than

TABLE 10. Overall assessment of the investment.

Factors	No. of Respondents	Percent	
Met expectation	16	47.1	Mean = 3.53, SD = 0.2
Exceeded expectations	6	17.6	
Failed expectations	5	14.7	
Highly exceeded expectations	4	11.8	
Too early to judge performance	3	8.6	
	1	Missing	

scale: 1 = Completely failed expectations, 2 = Failed expectations, 3 = Met expectations, 4 = Exceeded expectations, 5 = Highly exceeded expectations, 6 = Too early to judge performance

TABLE 11. Future plans for the Polish operations.

Future plans	No. of Respondents*	Percent*
Continue in present form	16	45.7
Increase commitment/holding	5	14.3
Change form of ownership	5	14.3
Change the line of business	1	2.9
Expand into other countries in the region	18	51.4

*multiple responses were allowed

50% planned to continue in business in their present form, while almost 15% were either planning to increase their holding or change the form ownership. In more than 50% of the cases, firms were considering expanding into other countries in the region. These findings show a positive and strategic commitment not only to Poland, but also to other countries in the region. Clearly firms continue to see significant market opportunities for their business or at least a viable secondary market.

CONCLUSIONS

While UK firms perceive abundant market opportunities in Poland, market entry to the country is not without risk. As a result, firms have made realistic risk-potential assessments, giving due regard not only to different types of risks, but also to the different levels of risk in their foreign market servicing strategies.

Primary data supports secondary source information that UK investment is spread across all industries, notably in manufacturing and financial services. While large multinationals are the single largest category in the sample, there are many small and medium sized firms, confirming the wide dispersion of business activity.

From the year of entry, UK firms appear to have adopted a cautious approach following the collapse of communism, and as a result, possibly have foregone first-mover advantages. Most of them entered the region between 1991-92, some two years later than their German competitors (Ali, 1996a). In terms of different entry strategies, many firms chose low risk methods such as exporting, use of agents, and joint ventures, apparently supporting international market entry theory. However, once experience had been gained, they re-evaluated their options and re-assessed the risk/rewards potential of their business, and made deeper commitment to the country by forming majority joint ventures and setting up wholly-owned subsidiaries. The significant factor is that change of mode occurred within a narrow timeframe, much shorter than predicted by established market-entry theory. Given that over 40% of the firms entered the market via wholly-owned subsidiaries, there is considerable evidence to suggest that, given the dynamics of Central and Eastern Europe in general and Poland in particular, traditional market entry theory may require a revision. The motives given as being extremely important for investing in Poland were unexpected, such as the existence of good local entrepreneur and following clients, the latter indicating the global nature of some businesses and the need to serve customers wherever they go. Companies had realistic expectations with regard to performance; the vast majority of the investments had met the firms' expectations and companies were optimistic to the extent that many planned to increase their holdings as well as move into other countries in the region.

From a management perspective, British companies' cautious attitude has paid off. Over two thirds of companies said that their investment expectations had been met or exceeded. This is good news for both existing and new investors in Poland, especially now that the country's economy is on a growth path. However, the initial risks in Poland and nearby East European countries (for which Poland may be an entry route) should not be underestimated by managers, who should learn from the early entrants. In this context, a close relationship with local entrepreneurs, in the form of joint venture and other co-operatives links, should be explored, especially by new entrants.

REFERENCES

Ali, S. (1996a), "German investment Strategies in Poland," forthcoming working paper, University of Bradford Management Centre.

Ali, S. (1996b), "Joint Ventures in Poland," forthcoming working paper, University of Bradford Management Centre.

Artisien, P., Matija, R. and Svetlicic, M. (1992) (eds.), *Foreign Direct Investment in Central and Eastern Europe*, London: McMillan.

Beamish, P. W. and Banks, J. C. (1987), Equity Joint Ventures and the Theory of the Multinational Enterprise. *Journal of International Business Studies*, summer.

Brewer, T. (1993), Government Policies, Market Imperfections and Foreign Direct Investment. *Journal of International Business Studies* 24:1.

Buckley, P. J. and Casson, M. (1976), *The Future of the Multinational Enterprise*. London: Macmillan.

Buckley, P. J. and Casson, M. (1981), The optimal timing of a Foreign Direct Investment. *The Economic Journal* 92, 316, 75-97.

Buckley, P. J. (1989), Foreign Direct Investment by Small-and Medium-sized Enterprises. *Small Business Economics*, 1.

Buckley, P. J. and Ghauri, P. N. (1994), (eds.), *The Economics of Change in Central and Eastern Europe*, London: Academic Press.

Casson, M. C. (1987), *The Firm and the Market*. Oxford: Basil Blackwell.

Cateora, R. P. (1993), *International Marketing*. Boston, MA: Urwin.

Cavusgil, S. T. (1980), On the internationalization process of Firms. *European Research*, 8.

Dunning, J. H. and Rugman, A. M. (1985), The Influence of Hymer's Dissertation on the Theory of Foreign Direct Investment. *American Economic Review*, 75 May.

Dunning, J. H. (1988), *Explaining International Production*. Unwin Hyman.

Egan, C., Shipley, D., Neal, W., Hooley, G. and Danko, J. Joint Ventures in Hungary: Expectations and Experience. *Proceedings of the MEG Conference*, University of Bradford, 1995.

Engholm, C. (1993), *The Other Europe*, McGraw Hill.

Falbe, C. M. and Dandridge, T. C. (1992), Franchising as a Strategic Partnership: Issues of Co-operation and Conflict in a Global Market. *International Small Business Journal*, Vol.10, No. 3.

Healey, N. (1994), The transition economies of Central and Eastern Europe: a political, economic, social and technological analysis. *Columbia Journal of World Business*, 29,1.

Harrigan, K. R. (1986), *Managing for Joint Venture Success*. Lexington: Lexington Books.

Hart, S. (1987), The use of the mail survey in industrial market research, *Journal of Marketing Management*, 3.

Hennart, J. F. (1988), A Transaction Cost Theory of Equity Joint Ventures, *Strategic Management Journal*, 9 (4).

Hennart, J. F. (1991a), The Transaction Cost Theory of Joint Ventures: An Empirical Study of Japanese Subsidiaries in the United States, *Management Science*, 37 (4).

Hennart, J. F. (1991b), Control in Multinational Firms: The Role of Price and hierarchy, *Management International Review*, Special Issue.

Hooley, G. J., Lynch, J. E. and Jobber, D. (1992), Generic Marketing Strategies, *International Journal of Research in Marketing*, Vol. 9, No. 1.

Hooley, G. J., Shipley, D., Beracs, J. and Kolos, K. Investing in Cherries and Resurrecting the dead: Foreign Direct Investment in Hungary. *Proceeding of the MEG Conference*, University of Bradford, 1995.

Howell, J. (1994), *Understanding Eastern Europe*, London: Kogan Page.

Johanson, J. and Wiedersheim-Paul, E. The internationalization of the firm-four Swedish cases. *Journal of Management Studies*, 12:305-22.

Johnson, S. and Loveman, G. W. (1995), *Starting Over in Eastern Europe*. Mass.: Harvard Business School Press.

Kim, W. C. and Hwang, P. (1992), Global Strategy and Multinationals Entry Mode Choice. *Strategic Management Journal*, 11:123-128.

Kaynak, E. (1988) (ed.), Global Franchising: European and North American Perspectives. *Transnational Retailing*, de Gruyter.

Kogut, B. (1983), Foreign direct investment as a sequential process, in C. P. Kindleburger and D. Audretsch (eds.), *Multinational Corporations in the 1980s*, MIT Press, Cambridge, Mass.

Lecraw, D. J. (1992), Multinational Enterprises in Developing Countries, in Buckley, P. J. (ed.), *New Directions in International Business: Research Priorities for the 1990s*, London: Edward Elgar.

Paliwoda, S. (1993). *International Marketing*, Oxford: Butterworth Heinemann.

Paliwoda, S. (1995), *Investing in Eastern Europe: Capitalizing on Emerging Markets*. Addison Wesley.

Pinder, J. (1993), The European Community and Investment in Central and Eastern Europe. In Artisien, P., Matija, R. and Svetlicic, M. (1992) (eds.), *Foreign Direct Investment in Central and Eastern Europe*, London: McMillan.

Root, F. R. (1987), *Entry Strategies for International Markets*. Lexington, Mass.

Rugman, A. J. and Verbeke, A. (1992), A Note on the Transnational Solution and the Transaction Cost Theory of Multinational Strategic Management, *Journal of International Business*, 23 (4).

Rugman, A. J., Lecraw, D. J. and Booth, L. D. (1985), *International Business: Firm and Environment*, McGraw-Hill.

Shama, A., Entry Strategies of U.S. Firms to the former Soviet Union and Eastern Europe. *California Management Review*, Vol. 37, No. 3, Spring 1995.

Strandskov. J., Towards a new approach for studying the internationalization process of firms., *Working Paper 4*, Copenhagen School of Economics, 1986.

Terpstra, V. and Yu, C. M. (1988), Determinants of Foreign Investment of CPS Advertising Agencies. *Journal of International Business Studies*, 19:1,33-46.

Tookey, D. (1969), International Business and political geography. *British Journal of Marketing*, 3:136-151.

Tovias, A. (1994), Modernizing Hungary's Industrial Structure: The Contribution of the EC. In Buckley, P. J. and Ghauri, P. N. (1994) (eds.), *The Economics of Change in Central and Eastern Europe*, London: Academic Press.

Turnbull, P. W. (1987), A Challenge to the stages theory of the internationalization Process. In Rossen, P. J. and Reed, S. D. (eds.), *Managing Export Entry and Expansion*, Prager, New York.

Vahlne, J-E. and Nordstrom, K. (1988), Choice of marketing channel in a strategic perspective. In Hood, N. and Vahlne, J-E. (eds.), *Strategies in Global Competition*. London: Croom Helm.

Welch, L. S. and Luostarinen, R. (1988), *Journal of General Management*, 14(2).

Williams, K. (1993), Can Western Investments in Eastern Europe Succeed? *Management Accounting*, 74, 8,17.

Wind, Y., Douglas, S. P. and Perlmutter, H. V. (1973), Guide lines for developing international marketing strategies. *Journal of Marketing*, 37:14-23.

Young, S., Hamill J., Wheeler, C. and Davies, J. R. (1989), *International Market Entry and Development: Strategies and Management*, Hemel Hempstead: Prentice Hall.

An Assessment of Foreign Direct Investment Opportunities in Hungary

Manzur Rahman
Claudio Carpano

SUMMARY. In this paper, we analyze Hungary's economic environment and locational factors, and their relevance to managers considering foreign direct investment in Hungary. Our findings suggest that, among Eastern European countries, Hungary is rightly the preferred location for foreign direct investment. In particular, Hungary currently offers excellent opportunities for firms attempting to use the country as an export platform and to firms aiming at improving their cost position. Over the longer term, we expect manufacturing firms in the high-end export markets to perform the best. *[Article copies available for a fee from The Haworth Document Delivery Service: 1-800-342-9678. E-mail address: getinfo@haworth.com]*

The level of global foreign direct investment (FDI) is again soaring, reaching a total of $226 billion in 1994 (UNCTAD, 1995). However, the competition for attracting FDI remains intense. While China continues to

Manzur Rahman is Assistant Professor of Finance at the University of San Diego, California. His research interests are in the areas of global capital markets, multinational financial issues, and foreign direct investment. Dr. Rahman teaches multinational financial management and corporate finance.

Claudio Carpano is Assistant Professor of Management at the University of North Carolina-Charlotte. His research interests lie in the areas of international management, global business strategy, and foreign direct investment. Dr. Carpano teaches business policy and international business.

[Haworth co-indexing entry note]: "An Assessment of Foreign Direct Investment Opportunities in Hungary." Rahman, Manzur and Claudio Carpano. Co-published simultaneously in *Journal of East-West Business* (International Business Press, an imprint of The Haworth Press, Inc.) Vol. 3, No. 1, 1996, pp. 63-77; and: *Marketing in Central and Eastern Europe* (ed: Jan Nowak) International Business Press, an imprint of The Haworth Press, Inc., 1996, pp. 63-77. Single or multiple copies of this article are available for a fee from The Haworth Document Delivery Service [1-800-342-9678, 9:00 a.m. - 5:00 p.m. (EST). E-mail address: getinfo@haworth.com].

63

be the black hole of FDI in East Asia, attracting in enough investments to be ranked second worldwide after the United States, the vast privatization programs underway in both Western and Eastern Europe also provide tempting investment targets (see the Wall Street Journal Report on World Business, 1995). As managers of the newly-invigorated firms from developed countries look to expand abroad, they need a systematic framework for analyzing the benefits and costs associated with choosing locations for FDI. This need is especially felt in the cases of the Eastern European countries that have recently converted to the market system.

In this paper, we analyze investment opportunities in one of the most promising Eastern European countries, Hungary. Hungary is located in a region of the world that is expected to grow rapidly in the near future. Assuming just a doubling of living standards and a completion of the major privatization schemes planned by the East European economies by the year 2000, it would not be unreasonable to expect foreign and intra-Eastern European investments in the region to rise from its 1990 figure of $2-3 billion to around $100 billion (Dunning, 1993). Among Eastern European countries, Hungary's stage of development is the highest after that of the former German Democratic Republic, which is a special case due to its reunification with the Federal Republic of Germany. Relative to other Eastern European countries, Hungary has the greatest chance for economic success with respect to: (1) economic development potential (i.e., industry structure, infrastructure, skills, foreign debt, and exports in convertible currencies), and (2) readiness and ability to change (i.e., commitment by people and leadership, and scope of reforms, experience with reforms, national homogeneity, quality of leadership, traditions/emotions) (Kraljie, 1990). As a consequence of these strengths, Hungary attracted more than 50% of all FDI flowing into the Eastern European region through 1995 (OCBA, 1996).

FDI is a function of countries' factor endowments and firms' strategies, where firm strategies can be categorized as market-seeking, resource-seeking, and efficiency-seeking (Dunning, 1988; Kogut, 1985). The remainder of this paper analyzes (1) the economic environment in Hungary with respect to FDI, and (2) Hungary's country-specific factor endowments. The final section considers the most effective firm strategies vis-à-vis Hungary's current and prospective strengths as an FDI site.

PROFILE OF THE ECONOMY

Gross Domestic Product and Inflation

The demise of the communist regime was followed by a high pace of economic restructuring that was necessitated by a sharp decrease in the real Gross Domestic Product (GDP) (an average of –4.5% a year in 1989-1993), rising inflation, relatively high unemployment (11% in 1994), and a large external debt (PRS, 1995). Apparently, the economic reforms were effective in promoting economic growth, and by 1994 Hungary had achieved a real GDP growth rate of 2.9% (IMF, 1996). This was the first growth in the country's GDP since 1989, and it is estimated that the growth rates for 1995-1996 range around similar levels (Lawday, 1995). Inflation, which had declined to 15% in 1993 from 40% in 1991 (PRS, 1994), is again rising: in 1994 it was at 19% and in 1995 it rose to 28.3% (OECD, 1995; *Economist*, 1996c). The contraction in fiscal policy throughout 1995 was aimed at decelerating inflation, which is expected to decline to an annualized rate of 20% in 1996 (*Economist*, 1996a).

Privatization and Foreign Direct Investment

Hungary has the largest private sector among the transition economies of Eastern Europe. Under the Hungarian Transformation Law of 1989 (which has since been modified several times), some state-owned enterprises have been transformed into shareholding and public-limited companies to facilitate their transfer into private hands (EIU, 1995). In 1993, private firms accounted for about 45%-50% of the country's GDP (HAEF, 1993). Still, by the end of 1992, only 17% of the state-owned assets had been privatized, 85% of which had been invested in by foreigners (EIU, 1994; PRS, 1994). However, the new privatization law enacted in May 1995, which provides a more transparent and streamlined legal framework to expedite the process, confirms the renewed political support for the continued privatization of the economy (OECD, 1995).

The flow of FDI into Hungary between 1989 and 1995 is estimated to be over eight billion dollars, which is 50% of the total flow into Central Europe, and greater than the inflow to comparable European Union countries like Austria and Greece (Houde, 1994; Lawday, 1995). In 1994, net FDI declined to $1.1 billion following the previous high of $2.3 billion in 1993 (IMF, 1996). However, a recent study by the European Commission estimates net FDI in 1995 to have reached $2.5 billion, and expects Hungary to continue to be the favored recipient of FDI in the region (*Economist*, 1996b). The sectoral composition of this investment is reported in Table 1. An analysis of the sectoral composition of FDI shows that most of the FDI inflow in Hungary was in secondary activities like mechanical engineering and machinery, chemistry and food processing (58%) (IDT, 1994). During the first half of 1993, the proportion of FDI in secondary activities rose even higher to 66% (EIU, 1993). The largest shares of FDI in the tertiary sector are in telecommunications (16%), financial services

TABLE 1. Hungary's Foreign Direct Investment-Flow and Investment-Stock by Industry.

Industry	FDI-stock[a]	FDI-flow, first half of 1993[b]
Manufacturing	58%	66%
Engineering and Machinery	n/a	27%
Food and Agricultural Products	n/a	19%
Light Industry and Building Materials	n/a	5.5%
Chemicals	n/a	3.5%
Energy	n/a	2%
Construction	n/a	1.5%
Trade		10%
Finance	7.7%	10%
Telecommunication	16%	n/a
Transportation	n/a	3%
Hotels and Other Property	7.5%	6%

n/a: not available

[a] IDT, 1994
[b] EIU,1994

(7.7%), and hotels (7.5%) (Table 1). The United States is the major source country with about $4 billion worth of investments (OCBA, 1996); other primary source countries are Germany, Austria, France, and Italy. Japan, England, Sweden and the Netherlands accounted for smaller shares of the total investment (IDT, 1994).

Balance of Trade and the Impact of Foreign Direct Investments

Hungary ran large current account deficits of 9.0% and 9.5% of GDP in 1993 and 1994, respectively. Clearly, such an imbalance was not sustainable (OECD, 1995). The 28% devaluation of the Hungarian forint in 1995, combined with a contractionary fiscal policy, reduced the deficit to a more manageable 6.9% in 1995 (*Economist*, 1996c). Multinational corporations play an important role in the country's exports. Affiliates of foreign corporations account for more than 16% of non-rouble exports (Morton, 1993 in UNCTAD, 1993). And in some manufacturing sectors foreign joint ventures now account for 25% or more of the country's exports (Dunning,

1993). It is through multinational corporations that Hungary can obtain speedy access to marketing and distribution facilities, particularly in Western Europe. Furthermore, it is the perception of a closer association with the European Union (including possible membership) that has encouraged a large number of multinational corporations to invest in the region (UNCTAD, 1993).

Hungary's principal exports are in: automobiles, meat, rolled steel, chemicals, machinery, textiles and others. About 50% of the country's exports are directed to Germany and the rest of the European Union (Lawday, 1995). In 1993, the European Union accounted for about 40% of the country's imports and the United States accounted for about 4% (CBM, 1995). The Czech Republic is also an important source of the country's imports (PRS, 1994).

The ability of the Hungarian economy to expand at a steady pace and the country's ability to attract FDI eventually rests on the quantity and quality of her factor endowments. These are discussed next.

HUNGARY'S LOCATIONAL FACTORS

Factor endowments have been central to the international trade literature since Adam Smith's seminal work. Smith had emphasized the importance of countries' differences in factor endowments such as natural resources and quantity of labor to explain international trade. Today, factors such as low-cost, unskilled labor and natural resources are increasingly less important than factors such as skilled scientific and technical personnel, advanced infrastructures, and the characteristics of a country's demand (Porter, 1986). But a necessary pre-condition for a country to be appealing to foreign investors, regardless of the quality and quantity of her factor endowments, is political stability. Therefore, we first consider Hungary's political stability, and then discuss her factor endowments.

Political Stability

Currently, the political environment of Hungary is stable (Lawday, 1995). PRS (1995) considers the risk of turmoil in Hungary for the next five years to be at moderate levels. The risk for FDI is rated A, suggesting that there is a very low level of risk; however, largely reflecting the country's recent, relatively large current-account deficits, inflation and external debt, the risks associated with financial transfers and exports are rated B. Thus, at the present time, Hungary's relatively low political risk gives the country an edge over all other Eastern European countries, and some Asian countries (PRS, 1995).

In 1990, the newly formed coalition government declared its goal to transform Hungary's economy into a full Western-style, free market economy. The economic restructuring process includes: privatization of state enterprises, reform of the banking system, comprehensive tax reform (took effect in 1989), elimination of trade and investment barriers, and liberalization of price controls (EIU, 1993). All price controls have been phased out since the last remaining control on natural gas was disposed of in April 1993 (EIU, 1993; PRS, 1994). Though there were temporary hiccups in early 1995 with last moment reversals on a couple of privatization offers, Hungary now appears to be back on-track with its economic restructuring (Beck, 1995).

Raw Material Resources

Hungary has almost no resource endowments. It is heavily dependent on mineral and energy supplies from abroad, primarily from Russia. While Hungary mines some low-grade coal and iron, only bauxite is available in large quantities, which has to be processed outside Hungary due to energy and technological deficiencies (PRS, 1994). Hungary is, therefore, unattractive to resource-seeking foreign investors. As a result, resource-seeking FDI is not present in the country.

Labor

The cost of labor in Hungary is low relative to Western economies. In early 1991, monthly wages were $140 compared to $235 in Portugal and $400 in Spain (Dunning, 1993); as late as 1994, monthly wages in Hungary were still less than $180 (IMF, 1996). The wage differential between Hungary and other low labor cost European Union countries was one of the reasons behind the decisions of many companies to change their plans and locate their factories in Hungary instead of in Southern Europe (Dunning, 1993). Factors contributing to the low labor costs are a weak presence of organized-labor and a governmental labor policy that is favorable to employers (EIU, 1993).

Supply of blue collar workers is two-tiered. Most of the unemployed are unskilled, while the work-force as a whole is highly skilled. Although the general skills of the work-force are good, most Hungarian employees lack adequate language, book-keeping and accounting skills. In addition they exhibit slow decision-making and bureaucratic management styles that are the heritage of many years of communist regime. These weaknesses may offset the benefits accruing to foreign companies as a result of the country's low labor cost, high level of the workers' basic skills and close psychological proximity to Western cultures (EIU, 1993). As a result, in some instances, losses from low productivity were greater than the gains from low labor costs (Okolicsanyi, 1992).

Western firms access the skilled segment of the work-force by paying slightly higher wages than domestic firms. But hiring the "right" employees may be difficult because of the low mobility of Hungary's work-force which is mainly the result of housing shortages (EIU, 1993). This is a problem especially for greenfield projects in areas with low labor supply. Although the future situation regarding mobility and quality of blue collar workers is likely to improve, the labor cost advantages, on the other hand, will possibly deteriorate during the next five to ten years (EIU, 1993). The reason for the possible deterioration is rooted in Hungary's aging population that will put under strain the country's socialized healthcare, her social-security system, and her program of unemployment benefits. The social costs associated with these benefits will be carried by the industry. Currently, employers have to pay a uniform fee of about 44% of an employee's salary to the state in order to finance these benefits (EIU, 1993). In addition, investors should be aware of the work-force's increasing dissatisfaction with a standard of living that today is below the 1990 level. As a consequence it is more likely that workers will seek the support of unions (EIU, 1993). However, a dose of reality has been interjected with the recent introduction of fiscal austerity programs, including significant cuts in social spending, by the Socialist government of Prime Minister Gyula Horn (Beck, 1995).

In summary, labor may provide foreign firms with a short-run competitive advantage in the international marketplace that is contingent on the skills that the foreign investors need and the obtaining of the correct location within Hungary. The advantages that Hungary at the present time provides in terms of cost savings are likely to disappear in the long run. However, due to its relatively long heritage of industrial strength compared to Latin American and East Asian nations, Hungarian workers can be quickly made competitive to Western workers in the high-end export markets by using better management. Examples of such turn-arounds abound in the consumer-brand packaging (Petofi Printing & Packaging Co.), liquor (Zwack Unicum), food processing (Goldsum Ltd.) and other industries that are already competitive with Western European firms.

Domestic and International Markets

Hungary has a small population of about 10 million with a relatively high GDP per capita of $4,000 (OECD, 1995); the National Bank of

Hungary estimates that the black market economy may add a further 30% to the national output (Lawday, 1995). It has obtained associate membership in the European Union and is aiming at establishing a free-trade area between Hungary, Poland, Czech Republic, Slovakia and the European Union by the year 2000. Under the associate membership agreement, the European Union has removed its trade-barriers against two-thirds of Hungarian industrial products; Hungary has a grace period of approximately five years to remove similar trade barriers. During this transition period, import barriers will be higher than export barriers to most European countries. As might be expected, this has had a positive impact on FDI. For example, Loranger Manufacturing Corp., a domestic supplier of Ford Motor Co., set up production facilities in Hungary following Ford's investment there. However, quantitative restrictions on European Union-sourced imports into Hungary were eliminated on January 1, 1995. This benefits foreign firms that, due to the lack of domestic suppliers, are heavily dependent on European Union firms for their supplies. All remaining barriers are supposed to be phased out by the year 2000 (EIU, 1994).

Hungary imposes virtually no restrictions and taxes on exports. Nonetheless, at the present time Hungary cannot fully exploit its locational advantages because of political and economic difficulties in former communist countries and because the countries associated with the European Union are not always fulfilling their promises to be open to Hungarian products. In fact, although the agreements with the European Union purport to remove trade barriers, recent developments dampen expectations for improved trade, at least for the medium-term. For example, the European Union has banned all meat and meat-related imports originating in any Eastern European country, including Hungary. In addition, Austria has limited the amount of chemicals, cement, steel, and agricultural machinery allowed to be imported from Hungary, on grounds of unfair competition by Hungary (i.e., low wages, high state subsidies, and environmental negligence) (EIU, 1994). By the time Hungary is likely to join the European Union, these problems ought to be solved and Hungary's attractiveness to market-seeking firms will be strengthened. Furthermore, economic expansion in the Commonwealth of Independent States may promote FDI in Hungary by foreign firms seeking to penetrate those markets (Dunning, 1993).

Finance and Banking

By 1990 Hungary already had an established, basic financial and banking system, which was in sharp contrast to all other former Soviet Bloc countries. The National Bank of Hungary is performing the role of a central bank. Reforms aimed at further deregulating the banking system and bringing it up to Western standards were implemented in 1991 by the Antall government (PRS, 1994). Although Hungary's currency, the forint, is not yet fully convertible, many elements of currency convertibility are already in place, and full convertibility is expected shortly (OECD, 1995). Concerns over the relatively high budget and trade deficits, and external debt, forced the government to devalue the currency by about 28% in the 1994-1995 period (*Economist*, 1996a); however, given official foreign exchange reserves equalling six-seven months of import levels, Hungary is unlikely to see a Mexico-style implosion. Furthermore, the 1995 budget includes significant wage, employment, privatization, and trade policies designed to lower labor costs and reduce public consumption, which are expected to retain the confidence of foreign investors (OECD, 1995).

A government securities market and a stock exchange were established in 1988 and 1990, respectively. However, many Hungarian firms are traded on the Vienna Stock Exchange in Austria (PRS, 1994). All foreign investors need to seek government approval from several agencies, and bureaucracy is often the cause for major delays in the approval process. This is especially so in the case of joint-ventures and acquisitions of large shares of Hungarian and state-owned companies (EIU, 1993). However, by 1996, activity at the Budapest stock exchange had picked up significantly, primarily due to the trading of foreign investors (*Economist*, 1996a).

Infrastructure

Improvements in Hungary's physical infrastructure have been substantial since 1989. Hungary possesses a good railroad system, a large part of which is electrified. Currently, the country is investing hundreds of millions of dollars on roads and telecommunications (EIU, 1995). The telecommunication system is being rebuilt and the state-owned telephone company, MATAV, has been privatized. As part of this privatization process, Deutsche Telekom and Ameritech invested $875 million in the state telephone company in 1993 (Perlez, 1994).

Government Policies

Incentives. Government incentives play an important role in attracting FDI. The Hungarian government has used tax exemptions, customs waivers, legal amendments, and government collaboration in the development of production sites (e.g., the construction of power lines and gas pipelines) to attract large Western firms like Volkswagen, Ford and GM. These incentives, in combination with other locational factors, such as low labor and energy costs, have resulted in relative cost advantages for many firms investing in Hungary, particularly in the automotive industry. However, primarily due to the pressure of domestic industries, beginning in 1994 the Hungarian government eliminated all tax holidays for foreign investors (EIU, 1994). The elimination of these and other incentives reduces the relative cost advantages for firms operating in Hungary, thus decreasing Hungary's attractiveness to foreign investors. The government has no distinct policies and incentives to encourage the development of any specific industry or region (EIU, 1994). This shift in Hungary's policy toward FDI may damage the country's long-run ability to attract FDI and to sustain economic growth, especially when considered against the policies of many East Asian countries.

Miscellaneous policies. The fact that intellectual property rights, such as patents, trademarks and copyrights, are well protected, especially by East European standards, is an attractive feature to foreign investors (HAEF, 1993; EIU, 1993). This protection reduces foreign investors' risk of doing business in Hungary, which is an advantage that Hungary has over other Eastern European and many Asian countries. In many industries, environmental standards play a key role in the cost of doing business; Hungary's environmental standards are low, a factor especially important to the chemical industry (PRS, 1994).

Hungary's current locational strengths and weaknesses as well as the expected future impact of current developments, trends and policies on these locational factors are summarized in Table 2. We believe that at the present time the country's political stability, educated, low-cost labor, financial system, and governmental policies toward FDI are highly competitive in terms of attracting FDI. Though, at present, we consider Hungary's access to foreign markets and infrastructure to be at a competitive disadvantage to the Western economies, these factors are superior to many other developing countries. Except for the obvious weakness in terms of lack of natural resources and the elimination of government incentives, we expect Hungary to be an increasingly attractive location for FDI.

CONCLUSIONS

The analysis of existing FDI and locational factors suggests that market-seeking and efficiency-seeking firms will find Hungary to be an attractive location for their activities. The trade data suggests that a sizable

TABLE 2. Hungary's Current Locational Strengths and Weaknesses and Trends.

LOCATIONAL FACTORS	STRENGTH/ WEAKNESS[a]	TREND[b]
Political Stability	S	+
Raw Materials/Resources	W	=
Labor	S	+
Domestic Market	W	+
Access to International Markets	N	+
Government Policies		
Incentives for FDI	S	—
Property Rights	S	+
Environmental Standards[c]	S	+
Finance and Banking	S	+
Infrastructure	N	+

[a] S: Strength
     W: Weakness
     N: Neutral

[b] +: Better
     —: Worse
     =: Stable

[c] Environmental standards are viewed as a country's strength if they do not require companies to incur meaningful costs to meet them.

component of Hungary's FDI is export-oriented. We expect this trend to continue. Since export-oriented FDI needs adequate infrastructure and service industries, it stimulates foreign investments in these sectors. The data reported in Table 1 indicates that a rather large part of FDI, about 58%, is in manufacturing industries that benefit from Hungary's locational factors. In addition, the data suggests that the export-oriented, efficiency-seeking firms have also provided the impetus for FDI by market-seeking firms. In fact, a reason behind the FDI of firms such as Accor Hotels, Sarp Industries, and Loranger Manufacturing Corp. is to pursue market opportunities generated, at least partly, by the FDI of efficiency-seeking firms. Because of the small size of the domestic market, it is likely that efficiency-seeking firms will continue to play an important role in the growth of the economy.

Table 3 shows the top ten investments in Hungary through 1995. An analysis of these investments reveals clear patterns (1) of firms investing with the objective of lowering production costs, and (2) of firms investing in the pursuit of market opportunities. The three firms in the automobile sector (four with Ford, which has invested $120 million in an automobile parts manufacturing plant) provide strong evidence of the presence of efficiency-seeking firms in Hungary. Similarly, the presence of four inves-

TABLE 3. Top 10 Foreign Direct Investments (OCBA, 1996).

Firm	Investor	Industry
MATAV	Ameritech (US) Deutsche Telecom (GER) $875 Million	Telecom
Tungsram	General Electric (US) $550 Million	Light Bulb
Audi Hungary	Volkswagen/Audi (GER) $420 million	Car Engines
Westel	US West Int'l (US) $330 Million	Telecom
Opel Hungary	General Motors (US) $300 Million	Auto Parts
Magyar Suzuki	Suzuki (JPN) $250 Million	Finished Autos
Pannon GSM	Scandinavian PTTs $250 Million	Telecom
Hungarian Biztosito	Allianz (GER) $220 Million	Insurance
Hungarian Euro-Expwy	Various (FR-AUS) $200 Million	Construction
KOFEM	Alcoa (US) $165 Million	Aluminum

tors in the telecommunication and construction business is a strong indication that the economic growth of the country is stimulating investments by those market-seeking firms whose products or services cannot be imported, but need to be produced locally. Further evidence of the market opportunities in Hungary is provided by the fact that both PepsiCo and Coca-Cola have invested more than $100 million each (OCBA, 1996).

Managerial Implications

FDI in Hungary is, as expected, heavily-weighted toward industries that benefit from Hungary's locational factors. These industries are characterized as being highly sensitive to labor costs and to high transportation costs, such as the packaging industry and the assorted suppliers in the automotive industry. Firms in these industries are mainly interested in developing an export platform for the larger European market. However, note that the presence of these efficiency-seeking firms has already stimulated an inflow of market-seeking firms.

Current policy trends, especially the elimination of incentives to foreign investors, and the standardization of Hungary's economic and legal structure to European Union standards will weaken two of the country's important strengths: low labor costs and direct investment subsidies. Therefore, purely efficiency-seeking firms may see smaller gains in the future. Similarly, in the short run, the outlook for market-seeking firms may suffer as a result of the austerity programs being implemented to bring down the foreign debt, and the budget and trade deficits. These measures may limit the economy's growth in 1996 to about 2% (Lawday, 1995).

At the same time, the country is maintaining its political stability. This will facilitate the country's entry into the Organization for Economic Co-operation and Development in 1996 (*Economist*, 1996a), future participation into the European Union, and her relationship with the countries of the former Soviet Bloc. As a result, Hungary should be an appealing platform from which to serve the markets of both the former communist countries and the European Union. Given the inherent strengths derived from an educated work-force and a strong industrial heritage, the incorporation of modern, Western management practices will allow Hungary-based producers to become rapidly competitive in the high-end manufacturing industries. In addition, foreign investors that face costs associated with importing most of their resources and supplies from abroad will see these reduced in the future with the advent of highly-competitive domestic producers of intermediate goods (Okolicsanyi, 1992).

REFERENCES

Beck, E. (1995). Hungary scrambles to revive investment. *Wall Street Journal*, *March 14*, A14.

Cross Border Monitor (CBM). (1995). *Indicators of Market Size for 115 Countries*. Vol. 3, No. 34, Aug. 30, 1995.

Dunning, J. H. (1988). The eclectic paradigm of international production: A restatement and some possible extensions. *Journal of International Business Studies*, *19*, 1-31.

Dunning, J. H. (1993). *The globalization of business*. New York, NY: Routledge.

Economist, The. (1993). *August 21st*, 1993. 18-20.

Economist, The. (1996a). Hungary: Knifeman knifed. *February 24*, 57-58.

Economist, The. (1996b). Emerging market indicators. *March 2*, 100.

Economist, The. (1996c). Emerging market indicators. *March 30*, 100.

Economist Intelligence Unit (EIU). (1993). *Investing, licensing & trading abroad: Hungary*. New York, NY: Business International Corporation.

Economist Intelligence Unit (EIU). (1994). *Investing, licensing & trading abroad: Hungary*. New York, NY: Business International Corporation.

Economist Intelligence Unit (EIU). (1995). *Investing, licensing & trading abroad: Hungary*. New York, NY: Business International Corporation.

Houde, M. F. (1994). Foreign investment in Hungary. *The OECD Observer*, *August/September*, 36-38.

Hungarian-American Enterprise Fund (HAEF). (1994). *Fourth annual report*. Chantilly, VA: Signature Printing.

IDT Hungary. (1994). Ungarische Agentur für Investitionen un Handelsförederung.

International Monetary Fund (IMF). (1996). Hungary. *International financial statistics*. Vol. 49, No. 2, February, Washington, DC: IMF Publications.

Kogut, B. (1985). Designing global strategies: Comparative and competitive value-added chains. *Sloan Management Review*, Summer, 15-28.

Kraljie, P. (1990). The economic gap separating east and west. *Columbia Journal of World Business*, *Winter*, 14-19.

Lawday, D. (1995). Survey of Central Europe. *Economist*, *November 18*.

Office of the Coordinator of Business Affairs (OCBA). (1996). *Hungary country commercial guide*. U.S. Department of State.

Okolicsanyi, K. (1992). Hungary: A car industry is born. *RFE/RL Research Report*, *May*, 39-42.

Organization for Economic Co-operation and Development (OECD). (1995). *OECD economic surveys: Hungary*. Paris, France. OECD Publications.

Perlez, J. (1994). Hungarian cooling to foreign investment. *The New York Times*, *May 3*, A12.

Political Risk Services (PRS). (1994). *Political risk yearbook: Europe, outside the European community: Hungary*. Vol. VII. Syracuse, NY: Political Risk Services.

Political Risk Services (PRS). (1995). *Political risk yearbook: Europe, outside the*

European community: Hungary. Vol. VII. Syracuse, NY: Political Risk Services.

Porter, M. E. (1986). Competition in global industries: A conceptual framework. In M. Porter (Ed.), *Competition in global industries.* Boston, MA: Harvard Business School Press.

Smith, A. (1937). *The wealth of nations.* New York, NY: Random House. (Original work published in 1776.)

United Nations Conference on Trade and Development (UNCTAD). (1993). *World investment report.* New York, NY: United Nations.

United Nations Conference on Trade and Development (UNCTAD). (1995). *World investment report.* New York, NY: United Nations.

Wall Street Journal Reports. (1995). World business. *The Wall Street Journal, October 2,* R1-R34.

Can Western-Style Marketing Be Applied in Transitional Economies? A Study of Consumer Bank Marketing in Poland

Jeanne Hill
Carolyn Kennington

SUMMARY. The authors report on research conducted to assess the marketing of personal banking products by Polish banks and determine whether Western-developed marketing can be applied in transitional economies. The study comprised three parts: interviews with senior Polish bankers to identify strategies, a survey of front-line staff to determine whether strategies had been communicated and reinforced in the reward system, and a consumer survey to determine

Jeanne Hill is Senior Lecturer in marketing and international business in the Department of International Business, Lancashire Business School, at the University of Central Lancashire, in Preston, England. She has worked for many years in advertising and marketing and corporate communications in Canadian-owned and multinational firms.

Carolyn Kennington is Lecturer in international business teaching on MBA courses for international cohorts in the Surrey European Management School at the University of Surrey.

Both authors have participated in a UK Know-How Fund programme to set up a regional management centre in Poland.

An earlier version of this paper was presented at the Third Annual Conference on Marketing Strategies for Central and Eastern Europe in Vienna in November 1995. The authors are grateful for comments both at this conference and from two anonymous referees.

[Haworth co-indexing entry note]: "Can Western-Style Marketing Be Applied in Transitional Economies? A Study of Consumer Bank Marketing in Poland." Hill, Jeanne and Carolyn Kennington. Co-published simultaneously in *Journal of East-West Business* (International Business Press, an imprint of The Haworth Press, Inc.) Vol. 3, No. 1, 1996, pp. 79-93; and: *Marketing in Central and Eastern Europe* (ed: Jan Nowak) International Business Press, an imprint of The Haworth Press, Inc., 1996, pp. 79-93. Single or multiple copies of this article are available for a fee from The Haworth Document Delivery Service [1-800-342-9678, 9:00 a.m. - 5:00 p.m. (EST). E-mail address: getinfo@haworth.com].

79

whether the strategies had successful outcomes. It finds that the concepts and tools of Western-style marketing can provide direction to bankers for strategy settings, but that successful implementation will depend on the adaptation of these concepts to the Polish context. *[Article copies available for a fee from The Haworth Document Delivery Service: 1-800-342-9678. E-mail address: getinfo@haworth.com]*

The transitional economies of Central and Eastern European (CEE) countries can offer unique and diverse challenges to theorists and practitioners attempting to apply Western business theory and experience.

The purpose of this paper is to assess whether marketing theory and practice developed in Western free-market economies is being used to help guide the strategies of firms in newer, transitional economies. It reports on research conducted on the marketing of personal banking products by Polish banks and finds that although the concepts and tools of Western-style marketing can provide direction to bankers for strategy setting, successful implementation will depend on the adaptation of these concepts to the Polish context.

The paper will first examine the environment facing banks marketing to consumers in Poland, and then review research on the marketing of banking products in other countries. The method and results of the current research will then be presented, along with the implications of the findings for bankers planning strategy and implementation.

THE CONTEXT–
THE POLISH ENVIRONMENT FOR CONSUMER BANKING

The state of economic transition in Central and Eastern Europe is varied both by country and by industry sector. The transition stage between command and free economies, while well underway, will take some time before the new market economies are stabilized. Many countries and firms seek the help of Western-style theorists and practitioners to guide them, but such consultants often find that the individual contexts present different challenges and require different tactics to achieve marketing goals.

Two of the key factors affecting the marketing environment in these countries are the privatization of monopolies without deregulation, and the hold-over of power from previous government-controlled bodies. These factors have key influences on customer behavior and therefore on the strategies and tactics that marketers would use in such environments.

A good example of this was raised by Kuznetsov and Worall (1995), reporting on a training provider in Belarus who did not market their courses because they needed only to convince the appropriate Ministry to recommend a course. On paper, the Ministry has no power to force businesses to do anything, but in practise it still dictates to those businesses under its jurisdiction, thereby providing the key purchase-decision criterion, and direction for the marketing plan. Hold-over power can also have structural effects on a sector: in the spring of 1994 the National Bank of Poland (NBP) salvaged a private bank which was about to collapse in order to restore confidence in the industry.

It should be noted that similar examples of these two important factors can also be found in Western countries with developed economies while transitions are on-going (e.g., the privatization of several monopolies in Britain and the continuing "dirigiste" policies of the French government). It does however raise another caution to those making judgment on CEE businesses and governments: neither side has a true market economy, and so prescriptions from economists and academics must be adapted to the case at hand in the relevant context.

The marketing of consumer banking in Poland is a recent development. As noted above, Polish banks do not face a developed market economy, but an economy in which market forces are beginning to be felt. There is a degree of competition in the market because of the de-monopolization which the Polish government has carried out in the sector. In 1985, there were two banks and a large number of co-operative financial institutions in Poland; in 1995, there were between 70 and 100 banks and over 1000 co-operatives, many of which are small and/or regional, operating in a medium sized market. One criticism that has been made of the way the government has handled the NBP breakup is that industry leaders believe there is only room for about four or five large universal banks in the Polish market (*Warsaw Voice*, 1994), rather than the 15 or so which resulted from the de-monopolization process. The result is intense competition to survive, and a growing belief that effective marketing may hold a key to success.

The uncertainty in the environment also has a great effect on the ability of these banks to compete. Established firms which are the banks' commercial customers are undergoing privatization and restructuring, and many of the banks "inherited" large loans held by these firms at the breakup of the NBP. The banks so endowed have started life with very unhealthy portfolios. In addition, the shocks applied to the Polish economy and the changes which continue on a regular basis do not easily allow planning as a business function: it is difficult for anyone to assess the future health of businesses in Poland and it could be considered that the banks are in the position of placing bets rather than loans. The high rate of inflation also means that the banks need to increase the value of their capital by 40-50% per annum. Because of the endowment of bad debt, the inheritance of staff and property and the changing legal impositions of politicians, most of the new banks are constrained financially, operationally and strategically.

Perhaps the most pivotal factor facing Polish bankers of personal products is that the concept of personal banking as we would see it in the West is new to Poles, and consumer behavior in this market is not yet well understood. A survey of Polish consumers (Hill et al., 1994) identified, among other things, that Polish consumers had relatively undeveloped recognition of the need for or desirability of new consumer banking products introduced by the banks. Three key reasons were that they felt they didn't need and couldn't "afford" such products, they felt considerable distrust of the banking industry, and they felt that the banks had not been marketing their products effectively.

The question which this article seeks to answer is whether marketing methods developed in the West can help Polish banks compete more effectively. As noted previously, deregulation in the financial services industry is not something unique to CEE markets but has been implemented in recent decades in Western markets such as the US and the UK. There is therefore a body of research which investigates how banks and other financial institutions have responded to the challenge.

WESTERN EXPERIENCE OF DEREGULATION

Research in the UK has found that prior to deregulation the banks focused on supply-side factors (de Moubray, 1991; Burton, 1991; Johnson and Scholes, 1993). The importance of security and control in banking and the relative protection from market forces allowed a culture to spring up in banks that has been almost exclusively internally focused.

In addition, the research has pointed out that banks continue to emphasize price and product in their marketing strategies, but de Moubray points out that price and product will not, in service industries, be enough to achieve sustainable competitive advantage. Whether this price/product focus will be possible in the future, or even the present, is a different matter in the UK. De Moubray (1991) notes that social changes have given consumers increased power in the marketplace. This power combines with deregulation and increased competition to threaten the position of the high street banks. His recommendation for implementing this demand-led strategy is through environmental analysis. Five broad streams of change are identified for UK banks: economic (consumers are richer); demographic (different consumers with different needs are increasingly important, i.e., older consumers and women); the role of the individual (responsibility and the need for dignity and respect); technology (access to information); and changed perceptions of security (increased concern with emotional and physical security). Planning which recognizes and acts upon these social changes will lead to greater success than planning which focuses on past experience and strengths.

In the Polish context all of de Moubray's five streams of change are important. The economic change in Poland is largely related to uncertainty and a major change in the distribution of wealth. Demographic changes have also occurred and the implications for the new distribution of wealth will take some time to be clear. The role of the individual is one of the most dramatic changes in the move to a market economy: Polish consumers now have great choice in all aspects of life and are fully responsible for the choices they make. Because they no longer have a guaranteed job at a fixed wage and products at fixed prices, Poles need to be more actively involved in managing their finances, but are suffering from the lack of knowledge, experience and information on their options. Technology and the impact of the "information age" are also viewed somewhat skeptically by Poles. In the past information provided by the NBP or other state institutions was as likely to have been propaganda as market information. In addition, Polish consumers are suspicious of anyone who wants too much information about their activities. Finally, the need for financial security is important in a market of such high inflation in order to protect the value of savings but so also is the need for emotional security in a world of sudden and bewildering change.

The application of de Moubray's recommendations in Poland would not be that different than for UK banks. Knowing and understanding the consumers is the first step and exploiting change rather than ignoring it will be the path to success. De Moubray contrasts the banks' understanding of the important consumer behavior variables for various products with a consumer's understanding: for example, the bank thinks "house purchase finance"; the consumer thinks "buying my home." In Poland a relevant example would be promoting fixed rate deposits vs. savings security. In the case of fixed rate deposits, promotion would logically focus on the rates. If the banks, however, were to promote savings security, competition should be based on satisfying the emotional and information needs of the customer and providing procedures which are uncomplicated and easy for the customer to understand. The key to demand-led marketing is knowing not only what the customer wants but also why and how s/he wants it.

Other research in the UK investigated which strategies led to success for financial institutions. Speed and Smith (1991) used peer evaluation as their measure of success. They found that the most successful (and admired) financial institutions employed strategies of high quality and controlled costs exploited through effective segmentation. The factors which were identified as increasing competitive pressures were similar to those identified by de Moubray: increased customer sophistication, deregulation and technological sophistication. The findings stress the importance of "knowing customers and knowing costs" (Speed and Smith, 1991, p. 29) and confirm Doyle's (1994) prescription of balancing customer satisfaction with cost. They recommend that banks segment the market rather than being all things to all people and suggest that an important method of implementing the segmentation is through differential positioning.

The need to control costs is also found by Thwaites (1991). Unsuccessful financial institutions are found to spread themselves too thinly across too many services. Recommendations include exploiting opportunities for differentiation in order to generate and sustain competitive advantages. Segmentation is further recommended by Philp, Haynes and Helmes (1992) who found that some groups, especially over 50s and women, were neglected by US financial services marketers. As noted by de Moubray, demographic changes offer opportunities for banks in terms of segmentation, and the research conducted by Philp et al. suggests that segmentation and differentiation will lead to success.

A case study by Burton (1991) of the efforts of a UK bank to change to a more customer-focused marketing orientation identifies obstacles to be overcome. In implementing customer service programmes designed to "put customers first," staff were given training and incentives, and were provided with information about goals and targets. Burton found that staff appreciated the information on goals and targets but that many employees were not comfortable with their new marketing roles. Their attention to marketing was seen to "interfere" with getting their "job" done. This implies that the implementation had not been thorough and that their job descriptions (or at least the employees' perceptions of their jobs), and therefore their performance evaluation, were still based on transactions or procedures rather than marketing or customer variables. Culture change in any organization is difficult and Burton's case study shows that job definition can be an serious obstacle. It will no doubt take considerable time and a holistic change in operating procedures and policies before the new marketing orientation can be fully internalized.

In summary, then, the US and UK research shows that there is agreement regarding the strategies financial institutions should adopt in a deregulated market. There is overwhelming support for differentiation and seg-mentation, based on environmental analysis, in order to increase the quality of service offered and to minimize costs, and for recognition of the importance of staff's view of their roles in providing that service to their customers, according to the customers' perceptions of needs.

THE POLISH CONSUMER BANKING RESEARCH

Research done in these and other markets would suggest that the ap-propriate use of strategic marketing would benefit firms trying to compete in challenging environments. Kotler (1994) identifies the three strategic tools of marketing as segmenting, targeting and positioning. One would thus hypothesize that banks which will be successful will be those who use strategic planning, based on a thorough environmental analysis (cf. de Moubray, 1991), successful segmenting of the overall consumer banking market, targeting of the most profitable segments, and appropriate posi-tioning of the offering to those segments. Because of the recency of the development of the consumer banking market in Poland, the rate of change in the Polish environment, the short span of time for which some of the banks have been in operation, the lack of information about banking consumer behavior and the lack of industry performance data, it is difficult to measure the relative success of the banks and their marketing programs.

In other papers (Hill et al., 1994; Kennington and Hill, 1995; Kenning-ton, Hill and Rakowska, 1996) the authors have identified key aspects of Polish consumer buying behavior relating to personal banking products and the most important selection criteria used by consumers to choose banks. The top four selection criteria were reputation, rates, convenience, and service. These are discussed later in this paper. In addition, they have identified the "wish list" that Polish consumers have for banks: the things the banks could be doing to serve them better. As well as items identified under the selection criteria this list included such things as more informa-tion, servicescape and keeping costs down.

The current research seeks to examine what the banks are doing to attract and retain consumer business, specifically:

1. To determine whether strategic marketing planning is being used, and if so, how (i.e., the use of segmentation, targeting, positioning and a marketing orientation).
2. To evaluate the effectiveness of these strategies as reported on by consumers and the banks' own front-line staff.

3. To investigate unsatisfied needs and opportunities for segmenting, targeting and positioning as revealed by a survey of consumer selection criteria.

METHOD

The research was carried out over a six-month period in a medium-sized city in Poland in which three banks have their headquarters, and many others have sizable branches. Studies were conducted at three levels so that results could offer triangulated cross-checks.

In order to assess the use of strategic marketing in the banks, semi-structured interviews were held with senior banking officials (presidents, regional managers, branch managers or marketing managers) in six banks of different backgrounds. For example, one was privately owned by an industry group, one was privately initiated, one was a universal bank created in 1989 from the National Bank of Poland break-up, and so on. Although the banks are different, they all face the same consumers in the same context. In addition, most of them have inherited staff and buildings from the NBP and thus the internal culture, as well as the external image, of the state-run bank.

There were marked differences in the respondents' understanding of marketing concepts and the use of an interpreter skilled in business, as well as in English, helped to overcome problems in interpreting the interview results.

The bank officers were asked first to describe how they perceived their bank's position, competitors and overall competitive strategy for consumer business within the Polish banking industry. This provided the bank's overall context and strategic direction.

To check for the key strategic variables, questioning attempted to surface the overall marketing strategy, articulation of a competitive advantage, segmentation, targeting, positioning statements and so on. Next an attempt was made to determine whether the banks were showing a marketing orientation or whether they were oriented to "product," "production" (process) or "selling." To determine whether the banks had an effective marketing planning process and marketing mix, the authors looked for evidence of environmental analysis, marketing research, planning and fully articulated plans making use of the "7 P's" of service marketing (i.e., product, price, promotion, place, people, process and physical evidence).

In order to get a measure of these strategies' effectiveness, it was necessary to go beyond the bank officers' comments. Given that these bankers were approaching the situation from the executive point of view, and given that there is often variance between what is intended by senior managers and what actually takes place at the customer interface, it was desirable to confirm that the strategies were in fact being carried out in practise and that they were seen to be working. Of course, for this to happen, the bank's front-line staff would need to be aware of the marketing strategies they were supposed to be following, and, ideally, their reward system would reflect the strategic priorities.

A separate study therefore was conducted of 65 front-line staff in five of the six banks (access to staff being denied by one bank). The paper-based questionnaire, distributed and collected by bank managers, was designed to determine whether senior managers' views of what customers wanted were consistent with those of the staff on the receiving end of daily complaints or kudos, and whether the staff believed that they were being rewarded for being customer-focused. While it was feared that the distribution method might prejudice the results, limited time dictated it as the only viable method. The results show sufficient "negative" responses to indicate that managerial interference was either not a problem or that the staff wanted to take the opportunity to let management know how they felt. The survey, which was largely open-ended, focused on four areas: image and strategy of the bank—what are they and how are they communicated to staff and the customer; areas of customer satisfaction and dissatisfaction; focus and appraisal of their work; and areas where the bank might do better in providing products and service to customers.

Of course, the true test of marketing strategies comes with customer response, so a survey of 205 consumers was designed to quantify aspects of Polish consumer banking habits identified in an earlier exploratory study (Hill et al., 1994) and to provide a mechanism for checking whether the bankers' perceptions of what their strategic direction should be were in fact the "right ones." This survey was mostly open-ended as the researchers did not wish to bias findings in a "new" market with Western preconceptions. For example, the criteria for choosing banks were all respondent-identified, and coded post-hoc, rather than provided by the researchers.

The consumer, staff and manager studies were all then examined for evidence of unsatisfied consumer needs, the existence of discrete and attractive segments to target, and key variables on which banks might differentiate and position themselves.

RESULTS

The Use of Strategic Marketing

The survey of bank officials revealed that the use of overall corporate strategic planning and particularly of strategic marketing was limited and generally non-differentiating. Two of the banks were focusing on indus-trial and institutional markets and did not have clear policies with respect to consumer business. Senior managers at four of the banks stated that their strategy and/or position in the market was that of being a universal bank, which is obviously non-segmenting and non-differentiating. In two of those cases their universal status was reported to be an imposition of the state. One bank did report a form of positioning statement, but this came more from the bank's overall mandate and ownership than from any par-ticularly consumer-meaningful positioning. Two of the banks seemed to be focusing to some degree on the price-sensitive end of the market and one marketing manager purported to be implementing a quality service differentiation. In the latter's bank, however, the general manager had articulated the bank's strategy as that of price-sensitive universalism, so there was obvious evidence of lack of coherence in strategic direction as communicated to (even middle-management) staff. (See Table 1.)

The lack of direction which the managers showed was confirmed in the front-line staff survey. At four of five banks over 50% of the staff surveyed did not know the overall strategy of the bank they work for or believed that their bank had no cohesive strategy. In the remaining bank, all of the staff surveyed were aware of the universal strategy, but the majority of the staff from this bank, along with those from most of the other banks, were not satisfied with the amount of information they received regarding strategies and policies.

The results of the consumer survey also supported this lack of direction. Depending on the bank, between 45 and 63% of consumers did not know what image the bank was promoting or felt there was no image. However, a match did occur between consumer selection criteria and the strategy put forward by senior management in that price and service factors were second and third respectively in the list compiled of consumer selection

TABLE 1. Awareness of Banks' Marketing Strategy

| Bank | Front Line Staff (n = 65) | | Consumers (n = 205) |
	DO know bank's marketing strategy	Satisfied with information on bank's strategy	Do NOT know intended positioning
1	13%	0%	45%
2	n/a	n/a	55%
3	28%	18%	46%
4	33%	17%	59%
5	44%	67%	63%
6	56%	29%	55%

criteria (Kennington, Hill & Rakowska, 1996). In this, however, Polish consumers are no different than those in other countries, as several studies have shown (Boyd, 1994; Stafford, 1994; Khazeh and Decker, 1992; Plank et al., 1992; Kaynak and Kucukemiroglu, 1992).

Evidence of a Marketing Orientation

From the interviews with senior managers it was found that only two of the six banks had conducted some marketing research. One of these banks places importance on service and staff training while the other had a marketing plan in place based on this research plus market analysis, SWOT analysis and so on. This bank was addressing customer retention through staffing and marketing tactics and was using some market segmentation and direct marketing. These two banks could be considered to be aware of the importance of customer service if not operating with a marketing orientation. The other four banks were focused on internal variables and their strategies were developed based on what they perceived as their competitive advantage, for example, price competition or new product leadership. In the case of these banks an internal or "supply side" focus to planning and strategy was clearly identified.

The results of the front line staff survey showed that overall, they felt they were appraised on control, transaction or process factors–a clear sign that a customer service orientation was not developed. In three of the five banks surveyed over 50% of respondents felt they were appraised on transaction factors instead of those relating to providing service to customers. In the remaining two banks, the figures were 30% and 40%, and a similar figure felt they were appraised on service factors. While this still does not equate to evidence of a marketing orientation, it does indicate the potential for development of such in these banks.

Use of Strategic Marketing Tools and Plans
Covering the Full Marketing Mix

As noted above, overall, the banks made very little use of environmental analysis, marketing research, segmentation, targeting, positioning, or marketing planning. An examination of the full use of the seven "P's" of service marketing revealed equally inconsistent and incomplete results in both the manager and front-line staff surveys. (See Table 2.) The most common preoccupation of managers was with price and most banks were also involved in promotion. Advertising (almost exclusively on price) was the most predominantly used promotional tool, but personal contacts and some direct marketing were also mentioned in two banks. Most managers

TABLE 2. Use and Awareness of Marketing Activities

	Proportion of banks (out of six) making some use of marketing mix element	Proportion of banks for which some consumer awareness indicated of bank's use of marketing mix element
Price	100%	100%
Promotion	100%	67%
Product	83%	50%
Physical	67%	67%
Place	50%	50%
People	67%	83%
Process	67%	83%

were also concerned with product–some in terms of universality and a wide offering of services, others in extensive new product introduction. Attention was paid to physical evidence in terms of improving or changing their buildings in order to distance themselves from the communist past and/or to give a modern or "Western" image. The development of distribution was an issue for three of the banks. People and associated service elements were identified by managers at four of the banks but this commitment was not clear to the front line staff surveyed. Process was also identified by managers at four of the banks in terms of computerization, cross-training of staff and the creation of new staff positions. The banks, then, are not making the fullest and most effective use of their marketing mixes, since the relative attention paid to different areas varies greatly and some banks are not using some of the elements at all.

The consumer survey provided feedback regarding the awareness of the banks' efforts in the various marketing areas. Awareness of marketing activity ranged from as few as three areas to all seven for one of the banks. While the interviews with the bank managers showed that there was patchy utilization of the elements of the marketing mix, the consumer results suggest that any marketing effort will be noticed and must therefore be planned with care.

Evidence of Unsatisfied Needs and Opportunities for Segmentation, Targeting and Positioning

The consumer survey resulted in a list of the selection criteria on which customers had chosen the bank services they now use. (See Table 3.) These criteria are discussed at length in another paper (Kennington, Hill and Rakowska, 1996). Analysis of the selection criteria shows statistical differences in the criteria for choosing banks for different groups by gender, income and age. This would suggest that it is possible to identify market segments based on their preferences, and to carry out meaningful

TABLE 3. Ranking of Consumer Selection Criteria

	All respondents (n = 205)	Rank Female (n = 96)	Male (n = 109)
Reputation	1	3	1
Rates (price, cost)	2	1	2
Convenience	3	4	2
Service	4	2	3
Only bank offering product/service	5	6	5
Conditions/terms	6	7	5
Family/friend influence	6	5	6
State guarantee	6	8	4

targeting and positioning against them. For example, although both men and women agree on the top four criteria–reputation, rates, convenience and service–there are significant differences (chi-square tests at 95%) in how they view three criteria. Reputation and State Treasury guarantee are more important to males, and family/friend recommendation is more important to females when selecting a bank. It is easy to imagine the differences in the tactical marketing approaches to these two groups that would address the different purchase-decision influences.

Similarly, statistically significant differences were found relating to purchase interest in specific personal banking products. (See Table 4.) Significant gender-specific differences occur for direct payroll deposit (90%) and car leasing/purchase (99%); age-related differences for installment payments (hire-purchase) (90%), and income-related differences on loans/deposit accounts (90%) and other, newer personal banking products such as stock market transactions and credit cards (95%). While some of these differences might seem self-evident (e.g., you need a good income to be able to get a credit card), some might need further exploration in marketing research to identify the reasons for the differences that are specific to the Polish context.

In summary, the three studies have confirmed that overall Polish bankers are not yet fully using the strategic marketing tools at their disposal, have not established internal marketing orientations, and are missing market opportunities in both their strategic and tactical efforts. The consumer study and front-line staff survey do however point out areas of opportunity to be grasped.

IMPLICATIONS

The research has shown differences in bank selection criteria and has identified the most important variables through open-ended questions.

TABLE 4. Purchase Interest

Product	Already use	Might use	Not interested
ROR	40%	23%	36%
Loan/deposit account	15%	31%	54%
Zloty deposit	58%	18%	24%
Foreign currency deposit	47%	25%	28%
Standing orders	25%	39%	36%
Consumption loan	6%	25%	68%
Leasing (cars)	4%	35%	61%
Payment by installments	14%	42%	44%
Mortgage	3%	22%	75%
Loans	18%	34%	49%
Other	21%	11%	69%

Indeed different groups of consumers can be identified and their needs differentiated so that the segmentation and targeting can be applied.

It appears that the banks are not making use of good differentiation and positioning, since bank staff and customers are confused about the strategies and image of the banks. Each bank's history and product offerings create some differences between them but given the large number of banks, the small overall market and the challenges of a changing environment, it seems that more substantial differentiation and positioning strategies must be indicated. How should the banks differentiate and then position themselves? Certainly there are insights to be gained from evaluating consumers' selection criteria, and, perhaps more importantly, their "wish list." Understanding the reasons behind the criteria and the components of the factors (e.g., "service" including knowledgeable staff, and being treated with respect regardless of "class") could lead to the identification of sustainable competitive advantage through positioning. Evaluation of the details of the environmental analysis would point out how to interpret such needs as security and respect.

As for research and environmental analysis, the research has shown that the consumer-meaningful variables for banking purchase behavior are similar to those in the West but have somewhat different meanings (Kennington, Hill and Rakowska, 1996). This means that further marketing research and environmental analysis specific to Poland should be conducted; this can provide the basis for marketing orientation (or demand-led planning) which will support the above recommendations for differentiation and segmentation. The Polish banks can also use this as an opportunity to gain a competitive advantage over foreign banks who may have an edge in resources, experience, and perceived safety and stability but who will have difficulty interpreting the environment and in understanding the consumers.

REFERENCES

Boyd, W. L., Leonard, M. & White, C. (1994). Customer Preferences for Financial Services: An Analysis, *International Journal of Bank Marketing*, 12(1), 9-15.

Burton, D. (1991). Tellers into Sellers? *International Journal of Bank Marketing*, 9(6), 25-29.

Doyle, P. (1994). *Marketing Management & Strategy*, Hemel Hempstead: Prentice-Hall.

Hill, J., Jedut, J., Kennington, C. & Zwierzynska-Coldicott, A. (1994). *Marketing Consumer Banking Services in Poland*. Paper presented at Third International Symposium on Management, Timisoara, Romania. Publication in Proceedings pending.

Johnson, G. & Scholes, K. (1993). *Exploring Corporate Strategy*, 3e, Hemel Hempstead: Prentice-Hall, 48-9.

Kaynak, E. and Kucukemiroglu, O. (1992). Bank and Product Selection: Hong Kong, *International Journal of Bank Marketing*, 10(1), 3-16.

Kennington, C. & Hill, J. (1995). Marketing Strategies in Consumer Banks in Poland, paper presented at the Third Annual Conference on Marketing Strategies for Central and Eastern Europe held in Vienna, Austria (November 31-December 1). Published in proceedings.

Kennington, C., Hill, J. & Rakowska, A. (1996). Consumer Selection Criteria for Banks in Poland, publication pending in the *International Journal of Bank Marketing*.

Khazeh, K. & Decker, W. H. (1992-3). How Customers Choose Banks, *Journal of Retail Banking*, XIV(4) Winter, 41-44.

Kotler, P. (1994). *Marketing Management*, New Jersey: Prentice-Hall.

Kuznetsov, A. & Worall, S. (1995). Cultural conflicts in a three-way joint venture: The case study of a marketing project in Belarus, paper presented at the Third Annual Conference on Marketing Strategies for Central and Eastern Europe held in Vienna, Austria (November 31-December 1).

de Moubray, G. (1991). Banking is Not Like Selling Toothpaste, *Long Range Planning*, 24(5), 68-74.

Philp, P. R., Haynes, P. J. and Helms, M. M. (1992). Financial Service Strategies: Neglected Niches, *International Journal of Bank Marketing*, 10(2), 25-28.

Plank, R. E., Greene, R. C. Jr., and Greene, J. N. (1994). Understanding Which Spouse Makes Financial Decisions, *Journal of Retail Banking*, XVI (1), Spring, 21-26.

Speed, R. and Smith, G. (1991). Marketing Strategy and Company Performance: A discriminant analysis in the retail financial services industry, *International Journal of Bank Marketing*, 9(3), 25-31.

Stafford, M. R. (1994). How Customers Perceive Service Quality, *Journal of Retail Banking*, XVII(2) Summer, 29-37.

Thwaites, D. (1991). Forces at Work: The market for personal financial services, *International Journal of Bank Marketing*, 9(6), 30-35.

Warsaw Voice, 15 May 1994.

Index

Albania
   economic chaos in, 32,40n.3
   marketization-Westernization in,
      34,35,36,37,39,40n.6
   urbanization in, 31,36,38
Association Agreement, 44

Balance of trade, in Hungary, 66-67
Baltic States
   Central Europe alliance of, 10
   geo-cultural sub-grouping of, xi,8
   Westernization of, 36
Banking. *See* Poland: consumer bank
      marketing in
Bosnia-Herzegovina,
      marketization-Westernization
   degree of, 37,39
Budapest stock exchange, 71
Bulgaria
   market reforms in, 32
   marketization-Westernization in,
      33,34,36,37,39
   religion of, 30,31,38
   unemployment in, 33
   urbanization in, 31,35,38

Central Asia geo-cultural
      sub-grouping, xi
Central Europe geo-cultural
      sub-grouping, xi,8
   economic development
      differences in, 28,32-33
   geopolitical characteristics of,
      35-36

   origins and language of, 29-30,
      31,38
   religion of, 30-32,38
   See also Region-relevant market
      analysis matrix
China, foreign direct investment in,
      63-64
CMEA (Council of Mutual Economic
      Assistance), 31,36
Coca-Cola, 75
COMECON (Council for Mutual
      Economic Assistance), 9,
      22n.2
Commonwealth of Independent
      States. *See* Soviet Union
      Republics
Conceptual equivalence of
      measurement concept,
      19-20
Confirmatory factor analysis models,
      20-21
Council of Mutual Economic
      Assistance (CMEA), 31,36
Council for Mutual Economic
      Assistance (COMECON),
      9,22n.2
Croatia
   marketization in, 35
   marketization-Westernization
      degree of, 37,39
   religion of, 30,31,38
Culture, definition of, 29
Czech Republic
   Central Europe alliance of, 10
   Hungarian trade with, 67,70
   market reforms in, 32
   marketization-Westernization in,
      33,34,36,37,39

religion of, 30,31,38
U.K. investment in, 50,53
urbanization in, 31,35,38

Deregulation
    monopoly privatization and, 80
    western experience of, 82-85

Eastern Europe geo-cultural
        sub-grouping, xi,8
    communism collapse in, 8,22,
        43-44
    economic development
        differences in, 28,32-33
    geopolitical characteristics of,
        35-36
    origins and language of, 29-30,31,
        38
    religion of, 30-32,38
    risks in, xiii
    See also Hungary: specific subject;
        Poland: specific subject;
        Post Command Economies
        (PCEs): Western research
        and application validity in,
        East European construct of,
        Region-relevant market
        analysis matrix
Eastern Orthodox Christian nations,
        9-10
Environmental dimensions of
        emerging markets.
    See Region-relevant market
        analysis matrix
Environmental standards, in
        Hungary, 72
Estonia, marketization in, 38
Ethnographic research methods, xii,
        19
European Commission, 65
European Union, Hungary and,
        66-67,70
Exploratory factor analysis, 20

Factor endowments, of Hungary
    conclusions regarding, 72-73
    domestic and international
        markets, 69-70,73
    finance and banking, 70-71,73
    government policies, 71-72,73
    infrastructure, 71,73
    labor, 68-69,73
    political stability, 67,73,75
    raw material resources, 68,73
Finance and banking, in Hungary,
        70-71
Finno-Ugric language family, 30
Ford Motor Co., 70,74
Foreign direct investment (FDI)
    in Central and Eastern Europe,
        44-45
    in China, 63-64
    in Hungary, xiii-xiv
    of U.K. in Poland, xii-xiii
    See also Hungary: FDI
        opportunity assessment in;
        Poland: specific subject
Functional equivalence of
        measurement concept,
        17-19

GDP. See Gross Domestic Product
        (GDP)
GNP. See Gross National Product
        (GNP)
Greece, Eastern Europe alliance of, 9
Gross Domestic Product (GDP)
    concept of, 20
    of Hungary, 64-65
Gross National Product (GNP)
    concept of, 20
    of Hungary, 69-70

Hungarian Transformation Law of
        1989, 65
Hungary: FDI opportunity
        assessment in

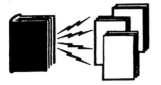

Haworth
DOCUMENT DELIVERY
SERVICE

This valuable service provides a single-article order form for any article from a Haworth journal.

- *Time Saving:* No running around from library to library to find a specific article.
- *Cost Effective:* All costs are kept down to a minimum.
- *Fast Delivery:* Choose from several options, including same-day FAX.
- *No Copyright Hassles:* You will be supplied by the original publisher.
- *Easy Payment:* Choose from several easy payment methods.

Open Accounts Welcome for . . .
- Library Interlibrary Loan Departments
- Library Network/Consortia Wishing to Provide Single-Article Services
- Indexing/Abstracting Services with Single Article Provision Services
- Document Provision Brokers and Freelance Information Service Providers

---

MAIL or *FAX* THIS ENTIRE ORDER FORM TO:

Haworth Document Delivery Service
The Haworth Press, Inc.
10 Alice Street
Binghamton, NY 13904-1580

or FAX: 1-800-895-0582
or CALL: 1-800-342-9678
9am-5pm EST

PLEASE SEND ME PHOTOCOPIES OF THE FOLLOWING SINGLE ARTICLES:

1) Journal Title: _____
   Vol/Issue/Year: _____ Starting & Ending Pages: _____
   Article Title: _____
   _____

2) Journal Title: _____
   Vol/Issue/Year: _____ Starting & Ending Pages: _____
   Article Title: _____
   _____

3) Journal Title: _____
   Vol/Issue/Year: _____ Starting & Ending Pages: _____
   Article Title: _____
   _____

4) Journal Title: _____
   Vol/Issue/Year: _____ Starting & Ending Pages: _____
   Article Title: _____

(See other side for Costs and Payment Information)

COSTS: Please figure your cost to order quality copies of an article.

1. Set-up charge per article: $8.00

    ($8.00 × number of separate articles) _____

2. Photocopying charge for each article:

    1-10 pages: $1.00 _____

    11-19 pages: $3.00 _____

    20-29 pages: $5.00 _____

    30+ pages: $2.00/10 pages _____

3. Flexicover (optional): $2.00/article _____

4. Postage & Handling: US: $1.00 for the first article/

    $.50 each additional article _____

    Federal Express: $25.00 _____

    Outside US: $2.00 for first article/

    $.50 each additional article _____

5. Same-day FAX service: $.35 per page _____

GRAND TOTAL: _____

METHOD OF PAYMENT: (please check one)

❑ Check enclosed   ❑ Please ship and bill. PO # _____
    (sorry we can ship and bill to bookstores only! All others must pre-pay)

❑ Charge to my credit card: ❑ Visa; ❑ MasterCard; ❑ Discover;
    ❑ American Express;

Account Number:_____ Expiration date:_____

Signature: ✗_____

Name: _____ Institution: _____

Address: _____

_____

City: _____ State:_____ Zip:_____

Phone Number: _____ FAX Number: _____

MAIL or *FAX* THIS ENTIRE ORDER FORM TO:

Haworth Document Delivery Service	**or FAX:** 1-800-895-0582
The Haworth Press, Inc.	**or CALL:** 1-800-342-9678
10 Alice Street	9am-5pm EST)
Binghamton, NY 13904-1580	